Finches

KARL PLATH

P. M. Soderberg

Distributed in the UNITED STATES by T.F.H. Publications, Inc., 211 West Sylvania Avenue, Neptune City, NJ 07753; in CANADA by H & L Pet Supplies Inc., 27 Kingston Crescent, Kitchener, Ontario N2B 2T6; Rolf C. Hagen Ltd., 3225 Sartelon Street, Montreal 382 Quebec; in ENGLAND by T.F.H. Publications Limited, 4 Kier Park, Ascot, Berkshire SL5 7DS; in AUSTRALIA AND THE SOUTH PACIFIC by T.F.H. (Australia) Pty. Ltd., Box 149, Brookvale 2100 N.S.W., Australia; in NEW ZEALAND by Ross Haines & Son, Ltd., 18 Monmouth Street, Grey Lynn, Auckland 2 New Zealand; in SINGAPORE AND MALAYSIA by MPH Distributors (S) Pte., Ltd., 601 Sims Drive, # 03/07/21, Singapore 1438; in the PHILIPPINES by Bio-Research, 5 Lippay Street, San Lorenzo Village, Makati Rizal; in SOUTH AFRICA by Multipet Pty. Ltd., 30 Turners Avenue, Durban 4001. Published by T.F.H. Publications Inc., Ltd. the British Crown Colony of Hong Kong.

Contents

Illustrations: Paxton Chadwick, 40, 41. Michael Gilroy, 17, 18, 24, 57, 58, 59, 62, 63, 64. Harry V. Lacey, 19, 20, 22, 23, 60. Karl Plath, title page, 4, 78.

Cover photographs: Michael Gilroy (front) and courtesy of Vogelpark Walsrode (back).

Tri-colored Nun *(Lonchura malacca malacca)*.

Accommodation

Anyone who becomes interested in finches, and finally makes up his mind to keep them, should first sit down and consider very carefully the question of accommodation, for unless this problem has been thought out with great care, the bird keeper will probably experience disappointment quite early in his career as an aviculturist.

Many who have made a start with bird keeping have given up the hobby in despair merely because they failed to think about the most important things first, in this case the cage or aviary in which the birds are to be housed.

Basic Principles

There are certain basic principles in the housing of birds which just cannot be ignored. Most animals, whether they are birds or fur-bearing creatures, must have the right type of environment if they are to survive for any length of time in captivity. There is also a moral obligation, and they must be provided with comfortable quarters if they are to be happy under the unnatural conditions which they are bound to experience when they are kept as domestic pets. The requirements of birds are comparatively easy to fulfil, and there can be no excuse for neglecting any of them.

In a state of nature most birds are accustomed to fly, and, apart from the breeding season when the hen has to spend a good deal of her time more or less immobile on the nest, much of their time is spent on the wing, even if it is only a matter of flitting from perch to perch. Thus, the area in which they are confined becomes a matter of considerable importance.

Birds should not be kept in cages in which they have no opportunity to exercise their wings. It is also essential that they should not only be able to flap their wings at will, but further, that they should be able to use them in actual flight. This must mean that there is an absolute minimum to the length of the cage from perch to perch. Now it is quite possible to keep birds for long periods in reasonable health in a small cage of no greater length than 18 in., but generally speaking, these small cages should only be used for birds which for many generations have been bred in captivity and have been bred in similar cages. Birds which come from the wild need a greater length of cage, and, although it would be foolish to dogmatize, 24 in. should probably be regarded as the absolute minimum for such birds. No one, however, with experience of birds and their habits would consider a cage even of this size as the ideal. It would serve its purpose, but cages of larger dimensions will be more satisfactory for all except the smallest birds, and probably for most species a 3-ft. cage is the one best suited to maintain them in good condition and to ensure their happiness, in so far as they can experience such a state of mind. There are some finches, of course, which can always be kept quite happily in small cages, but they are species which become so tame that they can safely be let out in a room where they can take as much exercise as they wish. Unfortunately, few of the small waxbills and finches become that tame and are also sufficiently intelligent that if they are let out of a cage they will learn to find their way back. If these birds have to be caught every time they are given their freedom, they are better in a cage all the time. Many birds dislike being handled and are terrified when they have to be caught.

With the larger finches, a 4½-ft. cage is desirable, and certainly no birds of the size of cardinals should be kept in any cage smaller than this. Thus, the length of the cage is of first importance because it is this length which determines the exercise they can take in flying from the perch placed at one end to that at the other. There may be other perches lower down near the food pots, but there should always be two perches high up which are as far apart as possible, as near to the walls of the cage as will allow a bird to stand on the perch without damaging its tail against the side.

Height is also important, but it is certainly not so important as length. A very suitable height for a cage to meet the needs of most birds described here is somewhere round about 20 in. A height of that order allows the birds considerable opportunity for flying from the ground up to the perch, and may

perhaps remove from them any feeling of being too closely confined. But it has to be remembered that upward flight in a cage does not require the same wing effort as horizontal flight. The distance from the front to the back of the cage, its depth, should not be less than 12 in., and would be more suited to most birds if it could be as much as 15 in.

Any cage which is 15 in. from front to back allows a shy bird to retire on the perch, so that it is not easily frightened when the front of the cage is approached by the person who is going to attend to its needs. Experience will soon show that there are certainly some birds which like to take the opportunity of getting out of the way because by nature they are timid, and these take a very long time to feel confidence in humans.

Cage Types

There are two main types of cage, and these are essentially different, but between these two extremes there can be, and often are, a number of variously modified designs. First of all, there is the cage made entirely of wire, which has been popular for very many years. The design of many of these cages is extremely decorative, and they are sometimes painted in gay colors to make them even more pleasing to the eye. Now there is no reason to condemn a cage of this sort out of hand, but few will disagree with the statement that this is a cage with very definite limitations. In the first place, quite apart from the point of view of appearance, there is no real value in having a cage of complicated design merely because it looks more attractive to the eye. Wire cages which are simple in line have a good deal to recommend them when this is the type of cage that is felt desirable. Usually they are rather on the small side, although many different sizes can be made to order. For most finches this small wire cage may have little to recommend it, but the fact remains that it is still popular.

One of the arguments put forward for the use of the all-wire cage is simplicity of cleaning, but if this task is to be really simple, there should be no fancy work attached to the cage at all, as one soon learns in practice that the more the decoration and ornamentation, the more difficult it is really to get down to the task of a thorough cleaning.

One very serious disadvantage with the all-wire cage is that it affords little protection to the bird from drafts which can be, and often are, fatal. Thus, if you decide that your finches are to be kept in a wire cage, then you must also pay great attention to the situation of the cage in the room, which will usually be the living room of the family. To hang it between a door and a window is to put it in the very spot in which drafts are inevitable. There are, in fact, many rooms in which it is quite impossible to put a wire cage so that it will be free from all drafts. If you

should decide that the only place for it is on a wall, then you have lost much of the apparent virtue of an all-wire cage, for you have actually provided it with a solid back.

Another point to bear in mind with cages of this type is that the bird is exposed on all sides, and there is really no place in which it can find seclusion. If people approach it from both sides and it is a timid bird, the possibility is that it will panic. However, there are many people who still believe in a cage of this type, and, always provided that they bear in mind its defects and the necessary precautions which have to be taken to protect the birds, there can be no justification for condemning such a cage absolutely. Usually one finds, however, that the person who starts off with a cage of this type in course of time is converted to the use of the other main type which is perhaps not so attractive in appearance, but which is regarded by most fanciers as more efficient. This second type is the box cage.

The Box Cage

This is a very simple cage in which the sides, top, and back are solid. Several inches at the bottom of the front are also solid, while the rest is made up of metal cross-bars through which other vertical wires pass and are soldered so that the whole thing remains firm.

Accommodation

Whether such a cage is made of wood, metal, or some other substitute material is usually not of very great importance, with perhaps one qualification. If the cage is made entirely of metal, it should not be used in a situation where the temperature can fall to a level below freezing. Metal is a first-class conductor of both heat and cold.

The advantages of the box-type cage are obvious. If the dimensions which have already been referred to are borne in mind, this cage provides a home for your birds which one can guarantee to be draft-proof, and in it there is much more opportunity for a bird to find comparative seclusion, if that is what it desires. A bird that is sitting on the perch as far away from the wire front as possible often seems to feel a sense of security which is never possible in wire cages.

It is usual to have cages of the box type painted on the inside in white and on the outside in black, but, although that may be the conventional color pattern, it is not necessarily the best, and is definitely not the most attractive. In fact, there is a very strong argument for having the inside white and the outside of some light color rather than the conventional black. Cream on the outside, with white inside, makes everything look so much lighter, even if this may be only self-deception. The paint used has to be carefully selected because there are paints which, if pecked by birds, may have unfortunate consequences.

Cage Bottoms

Whether the cage is an all-wire one or one of the box type, there should always be a removable tray in it so that cleaning is made a much more simple task. A tray is, in fact, quite a normal fitting for all cages. When this tray is taken out, it is a simple matter to remove the droppings and sand, and if necessary to wash the tray and dry it before again covering it with sand and replacing it in the cage.

Some fanciers prefer this sliding tray also to be painted, and if this is done, there are several advantages, particularly that of preventing rust. Generally speaking, painted trays have a much longer life provided that any bare patches are repainted as often as necessary.

Wire Spacing

For finches it is most important to consider the space between the separate wires of the cage. A normal size is 1/2 in. spaces. For larger birds, of course, it can be as much as 5/8 in., but even 1/2 in. is too wide for the smallest birds that the fancier is likely to keep. For example, the smallest of the waxbills, tiny birds such as the Gold-breasted, can, with uncanny skill, get themselves through a space of 1/2 in., and, if a window is open, they disappear, never to be seen again. Also, great care has to be taken to see that the fitting of the

Accommodation

perches does not increase the space between the wires.

Cage Furnishings

There are quite a large number of fanciers who make their own cages and aviaries, but perhaps a considerable majority of those who keep birds buy their equipment because they are not handy with tools. When this is the case, the arrangement of the furnishings is something which should be decided before a purchase is made. There are, however, a number of points to consider, and the beginner certainly must think about these when he goes to a dealer to choose any cage.

The two essential fittings are food and water pots. These should be of a type which is convenient for the person who is going to attend to the birds—that means that they must be placed where they are easily accessible, and be made of a material which is easily cleaned. Right-angled corners are much less easy to clean than those that are rounded.

Perches

The next essential for the cage is perches. Cage birds spend by far the greater part of their time on perches unless they belong to those rather unusual species which are accustomed in their native state to pass most of their time on the ground. However, none of the birds dealt with in this book is of that kind, for the birds described here are essentially perching birds.

It is quite natural, of course, that perches should be of certain standard patterns and sizes, but what also becomes quite obvious, when one thinks about it, is that birds are not themselves of standard size. Between the smallest and the largest birds dealt with here there is a great difference in size, which means too a very considerable variation in foot size. Thus, perches must always be chosen to suit the feet of the bird. It is just one of those things which one learns from experience by looking into the cage and watching the birds when they are on the perches. One can see whether they are grasping the perch with their claws and toes in a comfortable manner or not. If the perches are wrong, they should be changed without delay.

There is a point, however, that should be made here. It is that all cages should have several perches of different diameters. The largest, of course, should be of a size easily grasped by the bird without stretching its feet uncomfortably, but there should also be smaller perches. The reason is simply due to the fact that for a bird to keep its feet in the same position for hour after hour can become very tiring, while a variation in perch size does allow the feet to relax from time to time. Without doubt some of the best perches of all are tree branches. They are cheap and are usually easily procured. They have

Accommodation

the great advantage that when they are soiled they can be thrown away. It is a fact that birds which have natural perches and artificial ones tend to spend the greater part of their time on the branches, particularly if they still have their original bark on them. Hazel and willow are excellent for this purpose.

Seed Hoppers

There are fanciers who prefer seed hoppers to pots. Hoppers have the very definite advantage that, being covered on top, the birds are not able to foul the seed easily. Naturally, when arranging the perches, care must be taken to see that they are fixed in such a way that it is as difficult as possible for the droppings to get onto seed kept in open pots.

There is, however, one very distinct disadvantage with hoppers unless a good deal of observation is exercised. The idea of the hopper is not only that it keeps the seed clean, but that it saves labor in that several days' seed supply can be put in at one time. When this is done, there is a possibility that although the hopper may appear to be well supplied with seed, all that the birds can actually reach are the husks they have left behind, while they cannot, in fact, get at the seed at all. This danger can be removed by taking out the hoppers each day and blowing away the husks that have accumulated. If you neglect to do this, your birds may have days of frustration and hunger.

Aviaries

Although it is a fact that the greater number of finches are housed in cages, in many cases because their owners lack sufficient space to build an aviary, there are, nevertheless, many hundreds of fanciers who have a suitable garden in which a most attractive aviary can be built. Some of these may have no aviary because they cannot face the expense, but there are still many more who actually prefer to keep their birds in cages.

For the person who wants to breed finches, an outdoor aviary may be essential, for there are some species which are unwilling to breed in a cage in either a living room or even a bird room given over entirely to birds.

It is most important to make up one's mind as to the exact type of aviary that one wants in the garden, but before coming to such a decision, there are certain points which have to be borne in mind. Perhaps the most important of these is the health of the birds, for the pleasure or disappointment which the bird keeper himself achieves depends upon the fitness and long life of his birds. It is a fact, however, and one which has been learned through constant experience by those who have tried to breed some of the more difficult species, that there is little hope of success unless the breeding operations are undertaken in a well-planted aviary where conditions approach as nearly as possible the state of nature to which the

Accommodation

birds were originally accustomed.

The normal aviary consists of two parts, a flight and a shelter. The flight must be considerably larger than the shelter because it is in this section that the birds will take their exercise. How the space is divided between flight and aviary will depend upon a number of factors. In the first place, from the birds' point of view, the longer the flight the better, and if the aviary is a comparatively small one, at least four-fifths of the total length should be given over to the flight. But here a difficulty is created for the owner because it leaves him with a shelter which is very small, and from his point of view, attending to the birds will always be difficult unless he has sufficient elbowroom. In small aviaries of this type it is usual to gain access to the shelter by standing in the flight itself, for there is rarely room to make an outside door convenient.

Thus, probably the first thing to do is to decide on the length of flight that is necessary for the birds to keep them in sound condition, and then after that to consider the type and size of the shelter, each of which points will be governed by the available space and the cost. Many fanciers like their shelter in the form of a bird room so that when the inmates have been driven in from the flight they, the owners, can sit down and watch their charges in the inside cages or small flights. If a shelter of this sort is within the means of the bird keeper, it is certainly the one which will give him the greatest pleasure in his hobby.

Suitable Sizes

An aviary should be placed in such a position that the birds will get the maximum of winter sunshine. That does not imply that it must be placed in such a way that the sun can glare down on the birds at midday on the hottest summer day without their being able to find any protection for themselves. Birds love sunshine, but many people who are not fanciers at all will have noticed that in the full heat of a summer day birds seem to disappear. They like to get into the shade for a time, and many of them rest for perhaps an hour or more in the middle part of the day.

Nevertheless, sunshine must be available, even if protection against it when it is extreme also has to be considered. In the northern hemisphere, the aviary should face in a southerly direction. Probably it is better that it should not receive, over the whole length of the flight, full sunshine at midday, so it is often a good plan to face it toward the southwest.

The Flight

In exposed places it is unwise to have the flight covered with wire mesh on all three sides. If it is known that

Accommodation

prevailing winds which are cold come from a particular quarter, that side of the flight should be boarded up. In fact, there is probably much to be said for at least one side, if not two, being completely covered. It is a mistake, however, to cover the roof completely, for it is of great value to birds not only to have direct sunshine, but also to be able occasionally to let rain fall on their feathers. Very few birds like to remain out in a downpour, so to save them having to retire into the shelter, a small portion of the flight near the shelter can be covered over.

To be strictly honest in this matter, however, it ought to be stated that there are breeders of considerable experience who will not under any circumstances have any part of the flight covered at all. The beginner will naturally learn from experience which method of protection he finds more satisfactory in practice, but it will do no harm to start off with part of the flight covered.

Ventilation

Naturally, the flight provides no ventilation problem, but the shelter requires well-thought-out ventilation, with an inlet low down and protected against mice and an outlet on the opposite wall near the eaves. By careful thought inlet and outlet can be so arranged that there is no possibility of the birds being in a draft, yet it is most important that on hot summer days there should be a free current of air through the shelter. This is perhaps even more important at night when all the birds will be in the shelter. It is also an advantage to have windows that open. The window spaces must be protected by wire mesh so that the birds cannot escape.

At all times glass must be covered with ½-in. wire mesh because birds cannot see glass and will fly into it head-first and do themselves considerable damage unless it is made visible to them.

Popholes

The space through which the birds enter the shelter from the flight is sometimes called the pophole. Occasionally the word *bobhole* is used.

It is essential that the birds should spend the night in the shelter, and when they are unaccustomed to their surroundings, the task of getting them in is not always easy. For this reason a good deal of thought has to be paid both to the situation and to the size of the pophole. It is not unusual, during the first few days after a number of fresh birds have been introduced, to have to drive them into the shelter at night, and this can be a very difficult job indeed. Behaving from what can only be instinct, they always try to get as high up as possible. Normally popholes are not put right at the top of the division between the flight and the

Accommodation

shelter, but it is an excellent idea to have a hole here, either as a temporary measure in addition to the ordinary bobhole or, if one wishes it, as a permanent part of the arrangement of the aviary. Certainly it is far less trouble to get birds in when the entrance is right at the very top.

If birds which have been living in an aviary for some time are disinclined to go into the shelter, that is almost certainly due to the fact that the shelter is not light enough. Birds object very strongly to going into the dark, and so it is of great importance that a shelter should be light enough to attract them— so light, in fact, that they do not notice any real difference between the conditions in the flight and those in the shelter into which they are expected to retire at dusk.

There are various devices which can be used to shut the pophole, but by far the simplest from the point of view of the operator is one which can be manipulated without having to go into the aviary at all. It will not tax the ingenuity of the handyman, and certainly not the aviary manufacturer, to produce a slide which can be pushed across to close the entrance when all the birds have gone in safely for the night.

Doors

In most cases there is a door into the flight and another into the shelter. In the case of the shelter there is no real difficulty at all, because the birds are well protected by wire mesh. With the door in the aviary, however, it is another matter, and it is essential that precautions should be taken to see that as one enters, the birds, which may be temporarily frightened, do not escape. This can be achieved comparatively simply by having a low-down door, not more than 3 ft. high. When there is a door of this sort, it takes into account the normal behavior of birds, which are accustomed to fly upwards rather than downwards when they are approached. It may be a little inconvenient for the owner to have to stoop so low to get in, and the only advantage of a door of this sort is that it does save a little on the initial cost of building an aviary. Generally speaking, however, it is much better to have a safety porch, which is, in fact, a small vestibule, with its own door. The owner opens a wire-mesh door, goes into the vestibule, and then shuts this outside door behind him. After this is done, he is quite safe in opening the inner door which leads directly into the flight. When there is a safety porch, there is very little danger indeed of birds escaping when their aviary is being attended to, unless the owner is unusually careless.

Buying Birds

The only sensible approach to the hobby of bird keeping is to have the accommodation ready before there is any serious thought of purchasing any birds. It is more than probable that the species to be kept will have been decided while the accommodation is being prepared, but it would be unwise to consider taking delivery of the birds until full preparations have been made to house them.

It sometimes happens that a would-be fancier is presented with birds, and then his situation is somewhat complicated, for he just has to make do, and it may be necessary for him to improvise a temporary cage, but this is definitely not the ideal approach to the hobby.

There are various ways in which finches can be purchased, and there is something to be said for each of them, but here a word of warning must be given to the beginner.

Naturally some species travel better than others, and it is a good idea to know something about this before ordering birds which have to travel over a long distance. Such birds might arrive in sound condition during the summer, but could be in poor shape in winter. The best dealers, of course, refuse to send delicate birds over long distances unless they are quite convinced that they are more or less certain to arrive in sound condition.

Undoubtedly the best way of buying birds is to go to see them and to choose them. If an experienced fancier can be persuaded to make the visit and help in the choice, so much the better, but it often happens that birds have to be chosen entirely as a result of one's own decision. It is then a wise plan, when going to buy birds, to tell the dealer as soon as you arrive that you want to look round, and explain to him that if he is busy he can get on with his own work while you look carefully at the birds which interest you. A hasty choice is very often a bad one, and the dealer's time is valuable.

There are very definite signs of fitness for which a purchaser should look. Unless he sees these signs in the birds in front of him, he should come away without them. It is quite useless to buy birds at any time about which one feels doubtful, and it is unsatisfactory to the dealer who may later receive a complaint. To say the least of it, careless selection is unwise from the point of view of the buyer if he gets home with his birds and then, within a few days, finds that his new purchases are dead.

The experienced fancier is not unduly impressed by the feather condition of the birds at which he is looking. His trained eye may tell him why the birds look rough, and why perhaps they are short of feathers in places where he would hope to find them in full feather. The beginner, however, has not this experience, and it is wiser for him to make his choice from birds which are in excellent plumage, tight of feather and bright of color, if brightness of color is a characteristic of the species.

Buying Birds

In the case of the cheaper birds, the dealer will have a large number of them in his cages or small flights, a fact that does make selection somewhat difficult, but still by no means impossible. The first thing to do is to stand away from the birds and to watch them from a distance. Normally, if one walks straight up to a cage, all the birds in it immediately start to fly from one end to the other and suspend themselves from the wires, so that it becomes impossible to see anything except that the birds are alarmed and quite unnatural. Birds in that state give no clear indication of either health or sickness.

If one stands quietly some distance from a cage of small waxbills or finches, it will be remarkable if in a short time one has not picked out a few birds which are obviously alert and full of the joy of living. These birds are usually very neat and trim in appearance. It is a good plan, too, to keep an eye on the food pots. Those birds which go down to the pots and eat away with appetite are unlikely to be badly out of condition, but you sometimes see other birds which, although they are constantly by the seed and peck at it in a desultory fashion, do not actually eat anything at all. These birds are the ones to be avoided.

In practically every batch of birds that you are likely to see, one or two of them will be on the perches with their heads "under their wings" and both feet firmly planted on the perch. This is definitely not an indication of fitness.

They probably need to stand on two feet because they are weak.

It often happens that birds, when they first arrive and are exhausted, and probably hungry as well, may for a short time act in this way. If they are essentially fit, they should recover in a day or two. As soon as a bird which was in this condition gets to the stage of perching on one foot instead of two, then there is some hope for it, but even so, there is never any sense in buying birds which have decided to sleep during the daytime. That is something that does not normally happen, and the birds you intend to buy must at all costs be normal.

When you have watched the birds in which you are interested for a few minutes and have decided on several which you think are hopeful, this is the time to ask the dealer if he will catch them for you. Frequently this may be a difficult operation, but dealers as a class are skillful at catching birds and will quite definitely pick out some of the birds you have chosen. You should then inspect them in a smaller cage, for when they can be seen in this fashion at close quarters there are other signs of fitness or ill health which ought to become apparent.

First of all, the eyes should be inspected very carefully. The bird with a bright and clean eye probably has very little wrong with it, but if the eyes are watery or there is any discharge of any kind, or, as often happens, one eye is closed, then such birds should be

Buying Birds

returned to the stock cage from which they were selected.

After a few minutes you will have reduced the number of your first selection to just a few birds, and you can probably pick out the pair which you feel you would like to have. However, before you actually agree to buy them, you should ask the dealer to get them out and hold them in his hand for you so that you can look at the vent. If the vent is gummed up, which in itself may not indicate any serious disease, there is still no need to take any chances. A clean vent is always preferable to one that is dirty. The experienced fancier, by looking at the vent, can often tell whether the trouble is the result of digestive disorder or merely that the bird has got soiled through the fact that it has probably been kept under crowded conditions in an unsuitable travelling box. The beginner does not possess this skill.

The next thing to do is to look at the feet, because so often birds which are imported are found to have defective feet. It may sound rather stupid, but it is important that you should actually make sure that all the toes are present, for a sound pair of feet is an essential. Swollen feet are also an indication that something may be wrong, but this condition is met with much more frequently in the case of softbills than with hardbills, which the seedeaters are.

Having at last decided on the birds you intend to purchase, you will have them packed in a suitable box and will get them home as quickly as you can. Should you have other birds, you will see that the new arrivals are kept by themselves for a few weeks. Particularly in the case of newly imported birds, there is always the risk of infectious disease, and it would be the height of folly to introduce this to birds which are healthy. Thus, temporary isolation of new purchases is just plain common sense.

Acclimation

The word *acclimation* really means much more than getting exotic birds used to a northern climate. Adjustment to unusual temperatures is, of course, important for some species which come from tropical lands and are delicate, but generally speaking the word implies a method of treatment which allows these birds to become

---

Photographs, pages 17-24: 17—White-breasted Gouldian Finch cock (Chloebia gouldiae). 18—African Silverbill (Lonchura cantans). 19—Black-headed Nuns (Lonchura malacca atricapilla). 20—Peters's Twinspot cock (Hypargos niveoguttatus). 22—Common (St. Helena) Waxbills (Estrilda astrild). 23—Red Avadavat (Strawberry Finch) pair (Amandava amandava). 24—Long-tailed Grass-Finch (Poephila acuticauda hecki).

accustomed to an environment which is entirely different from that which they have experienced in their native haunts. Few species which are imported into this country can be provided with exactly the same food which it has been their habit to find for themselves in their own country, and it thus becomes the task of the person who is acclimating them to get them onto those foods for captive birds which will be easily available.

A further point to remember is that until they were trapped and transported to dealers, these birds have had no limit of any kind put on their freedom. When first placed in cages, they are naturally easily alarmed, and it is only by the patience of the person who is looking after them that they will, in a comparatively short space of time, settle down and become steady. For this purpose it is a sound idea to put exotic birds in comparatively small cages at first. The dealer cannot afford either the space or the cages for such care, but the purchaser who is the bird fancier will find that many species which are extremely wild when he first gets them become reasonably tame if they are treated with care and consideration, and also if a determined and patient attempt is made to win their confidence. The period of time spent in a cage is valuable too in that it allows the owner to inspect the birds very carefully for possible signs of ill health.

Another aspect of acclimation is that it provides isolation from birds which

have been in the fancier's possession for some time and are known to be fit. There are a number of bird diseases which do not immediately show themselves, and two to three weeks in a cage as a minimum will ensure that the new birds, when they are finally added to a collection, will be unlikely to be carriers of disease.

Generally speaking, temperature is not of great importance as far as the seed eaters are concerned, provided that they are not subjected to extreme cold. Many of them come from tropical countries where the day temperature reaches a very high level, but they have, during their short lives, grown accustomed to the rapid and considerable falls in temperature which occur at night. Ordinary living-room temperatures are quite satisfactory for most seed-eating species.

Were it possible, it would always be wise to import birds in the spring, so that after a space of a few weeks in which to settle them down and to allow them to become accustomed to unusual foods, they could be put outside in the aviary or mixed with established birds in the cages of the bird room. Unfortunately, that is not always possible, for there are countries which have a closed season for the export of birds. In these countries they may not be trapped during the breeding season, which means that they have to come into this country at a period of the year when the weather generally will be against them if they have come from the

Buying Birds

tropics. However, a little thought and some experience will soon teach the bird keeper how to deal with those new birds which reach him at a time of year which he would normally consider to be unsatisfactory. The species, however, which are so delicate that they cannot be handled by the bird keeper of some moderate general experience are few in number.

There are quite a large number of species which are frequently imported, are cheap in price, and present no acclimating difficulty at all. There are also others which are so much more expensive that the fancier feels that he wants to take particular care of them so that there shall be few losses. It is an entirely mistaken idea, however, to think that any exotic birds need coddling, for coddling never produces hardiness. Some birds are hardy by nature, whereas others are delicate, but all of them, if they are to be satisfactory inmates of cage or aviary, must be hardened off so that they can endure the conditions of captivity without serious discomfort. Very few species are so difficult that this aim cannot be achieved after careful thought and attention to detail.

One fact must be accepted. It is that how the birds are treated when they first come into the country does have a lasting effect upon them. If they are acclimated carefully, there should be no further trouble at all, and these birds ought to live far longer than they would be likely to do even if they were left in freedom in the wild.

Perhaps the proof of satisfactory treatment of newly imported birds is how they fare during their first molt in captivity. That is very often a critical time, but if it is surmounted without undue difficulty, then from that time onward there should be no further trouble, provided that sound common-sense methods are the normal practice of the fancier. No matter what the species, carelessness and a failure to attend to detail always bring in train inevitable disappointment and disaster.

Recently transported birds which arrive exhausted should always be put in a temperature higher than that which will later be normal for them. For several days they may have been short of food, and they will have no body heat to spare.

As wide a variety as possible of suitable foods should be put before them, and this food must be placed where the birds are bound to see it. Several pots are certainly better than one at this time, and the same remark also applies to water pots.

It is usually a good idea not to provide baths at first, but to wait until the birds are seen trying to bathe in their water pots.

For the first day or two the cages in which new birds are housed should only be approached when necessary; but when they are eating well, the same care not to alarm them will be unnecessary, for by this time the business of acclimation will be well underway.

Food and Water

It is impossible to overemphasize the importance of water in bird keeping because all birds, unless they are almost entirely fruit eaters, insectivores, or nectar feeders, drink quite a considerable quantity of water in the course of a day. Naturally, during those times of the year when there is a wide variety of popular green food available, the amount of water needed will be less. However, even so, perhaps even more important than clean seed is fresh drinking water, which should be kept in pots which cannot possibly become fouled. Water into which the droppings of birds fall becomes a very probable source of disease if at any time there is any infection among the birds.

The position of the water pots is also important for another reason, because the birds soon show that water which has been allowed to stand for some hours in full sunshine is much less palatable than that which has been kept in the shade. At all times water pots should be filled at least once a day, and, during hot weather, it is a good idea to give water as many times as is convenient. When the water pot is emptied, it should always be cleaned before it is refilled.

Water is also valuable for another reason based on the fact that it is the natural instinct of birds to bathe. The majority of birds which are kept in captivity enjoy bathing, and some of them are prepared to soak themselves many times during the day. It may perhaps seem strange, but birds as an animal group appear to be extremely particular about the cleanliness of the water which they use for bathing, and they object to bathing in dirty water and will only do so if no other is available.

In an aviary it is usually extremely simple to put a large dish on a stand, and it is interesting from the point of view of the owner to stand by and watch his birds bathing themselves, and then afterwards preening their feathers with great vigor and thoroughness. No bird ever looks in really fine feather unless it gets an opportunity to wash itself and then to carry out this specialized toilet with its beak.

For birds that are kept in cages, it is possible to buy baths which can be fitted onto the door of the cage. Baths of this sort probably have the advantage that they prevent the bottom of the cage from getting as wet as it otherwise would, but many birds are not inclined to bathe in a receptacle which is outside the cage because, to them, it is too exposed and therefore dangerous.

Although most species are truly enthusiastic bathers, there are individual birds which object very strongly to getting into the water which is provided for them, probably because they have some suspicion of the container. When that is the case, they have to be sprayed. During the winter time they should still be sprayed, but if the birds are at all delicate, with water that is really hot. By the time this water has been atomized to a very fine spray it is not at

Food and Water

all hot, and will certainly do no harm. Cold water, on the other hand, may produce a chill. Some of the more hardy species are even prepared to break thin ice so that they can enjoy their daily bath.

A word of warning must be given here about winter bathing in really cold weather. If the temperature of the shelter is low, only those birds should be allowed to bathe which are known to be very active after they have performed their ablutions. Delicate birds will have a heated shelter, so this problem will not arise.

Feeding

The importance of correct feeding for finches, and particularly the comparatively small ones dealt with in this book, cannot be overemphasized, for, to mention one point alone, their resistance is quickly lowered if the diet they receive is unsatisfactory. Lowered resistance produced by malnutrition means that they are more likely to develop diseases of various kinds, and all who have kept small birds must have realized how quickly they can die when they are out of condition. In fact, it does happen that a bird suddenly becomes ill and is dead before one can do anything at all to help it. It is, however, a cheering fact that sound condition can be promoted by right methods of feeding. The experienced fancier has learned this fact very early

on in his career, but there is no reason at all why the beginner should not have at his disposal sufficient information to make it possible for him to feed his birds on the right lines from the start.

The satisfactory nutrition of birds is a complicated business scientifically, but quite simply it means that different types of feeding matter must be present in the diet that is provided. Certain elements are essential for correct feeding. The word *element* is not used in its scientific sense, but is an expression to cover the different types of food which may be found in a particular item of diet: the carbohydrates, the proteins, the fats, the vitamins, the minerals—all of which in one way or another are essential to good health. Very few foods contain all these groups, but a variety of foods can cover the whole list. Now it is not necessary for the bird fancier to sit down to calculate calories, which is often the lot of those who have to feed human beings, because in the case of birds correct feeding can usually be achieved by providing a wide variety of different foods. The wider this variety, the greater the chance that all the essentials of correct feeding will have been covered.

When talking of the feeding of birds, one rarely considers how much food should be given, for the simple reason that there is always a tendency to put before them more than an adequate supply. Thus, the only caution that has to be given from time to time is that

28

Food and Water

certain items of food should be limited in quantity, usually because of their fattening effect—an effect which will not be as noticeable with birds which have ample exercise as with those which are confined in a comparatively small space.

Seeds

All the birds dealt with in this book are seed eaters. That does not mean that they eat nothing but seed, but their main item of diet is seed, usually consisting of several different kinds. Birds have their likes and dislikes and usually show a preference for one type of seed over some of the others. Thus, it is a sound idea to provide the seeds which are suited to the inmates of either cage or aviary in separate pots so that the birds can take what they want without having to search through the mixture to find what they like, and throw out, as they will do, what they have no use for at the moment. There are many fanciers who do not believe in separate pots for seeds, and if anyone feels that way he can put his mixture in the pots. Perhaps he has no need to worry unduly about the seed which gets thrown onto the floor of the cage or the aviary, for the chances are that where a number of birds are kept together what one bird wastes another bird may immediately pick up.

The quality of the seed provided for birds is of great importance, and it is always wiser to go to dealers who are known to be very careful preparers of seed. If only one or two birds are kept, it is probable that the seed mixture will be bought packaged, and packaged seeds are usually prepared by firms who have great experience and, perhaps even more important, a long-standing reputation to maintain. Dirty seed is always dangerous, and so care should be taken to see that any seed mixture has been carefully cleaned, and anything which could have contaminated it has been removed.

Varieties of Seeds

One of the most popular seeds is small yellow millet. It is this seed which is extremely popular with even the smallest birds, and they will eat it usually in preference to anything else.

The larger white millet is also valuable, and is a great favorite with birds which are able to husk it easily. The smallest birds find it very difficult to remove the husks from white millet, and for this reason are inclined to ignore it. It is, however, a valuable food because there is much more kernel than husk.

Canary seed is also another great favorite with those birds which have either known it in the wild or have quickly learned to appreciate it in captivity. Canary is grown in various parts of the world, and quality and size vary considerably. Some of the birds which are dealt with here cannot

Food and Water

manage the biggest varieties of canary but get on very well with those which are smaller. It has a very high feeding value.

Millet in spray form may be rather expensive, but it is well worth feeding to all exotic seed eaters. If they have the choice of millet in a pot or millet in the spray in which it was grown, they will certainly choose the spray first. From experience bird fanciers have found that spray millet is a great conditioner.

It is usual to feed the seeds which have already been mentioned in a dry state, but there is something to be said for providing sprouted seed also. Many birds in the wild like to scratch about on the ground and to pick up seed which has dropped from grasses and has started to germinate in the ground. Seed in this state is certainly richer in vitamins than dried seed, but it does lose some of its protein value when it has sprouted.

Particularly during the winter-time, when green food may be short, there is a very strong argument for feeding sprouted seed from time to time. The actual business of sprouting is not at all difficult.

There are fanciers who throw down seed on the floor of their aviary, where in time some of it germinates and is picked up by the birds. There are birds, in fact, which prefer to pick up their food from the ground, but on the whole, unless one can be quite sure that the seed thrown down is not likely to be polluted by the birds' droppings, this method of feeding has little to recommend it.

Hemp is another seed which is used for the larger birds, but should only be given in small quantities. Birds of the size of sparrows and larger can also deal with crushed oats, and there are just a few species which are very difficult to get on to the more ordinary seeds unless first they have an opportunity also of eating paddy rice. This is rice in its natural state in the husk, and is the seed to which they have been accustomed.

The largest of the birds mentioned here will appreciate hulled sunflower seed, occasionally. There is a tendency for all seeds to deteriorate the longer they are kept, and there is definitely sound sense in getting a supply of the new season's crop every year.

Green Food

Most birds will eat green food, although there are a few species which seem to take no interest in it at all. Yet, if finches can be persuaded to take green food, it will certainly be to their physical advantage. The most popular form of green food is seeding grasses, and for certain periods of the year it is a comparatively simple matter to provide a number of different varieties of such grasses, and to tie them in bunches to be suspended in either the aviary or the cage where the birds can get at them easily. Probably the two most popular wild grasses are poa and rye.

Food and Water

Unfortunately, seeding grasses are not available all the year round, and the fancier is compelled to rely on substitute green foods, some of which are, however, quite popular. Spinach and spinach beet are frequently eaten with eagerness, and lettuce, although it is doubtful whether it has a great deal of feeding value, is rarely neglected by birds that like green food with fleshy leaves. Those garden greens which have been sprayed with various chemicals should be regarded with suspicion.

Whole books have been written on the subject of wild green foods which can be used in the feeding of birds, and those who are interested should obtain such books to see what a wide variety the countryside can provide for their birds. Chickweed, groundsel, dandelion, and plantain are usually obtainable by anybody who does not live in the heart of a town. Some care must be taken to see that the wild green foods which are obtained have not been soiled by cats or dogs. That is a task which is not difficult to achieve if one takes the trouble to collect these foods well away from the roadside.

Many birds are thrilled when a turf is put into their cage or aviary, particularly if the aviary happens to be one with a concrete floor. They not only like to eat the grass, but if it is wet, many birds will bathe themselves in it after they have finished eating all they need for the moment. A fresh turf several times a week is easily obtained, and gives the birds pleasure as well as providing some small part of their diet.

Seed-eating birds on the whole are not fruit eaters, but quite a number of species will eat apple, and some of them will even eat the more fleshy fruits. One never knows what one's birds will eat of foods of this sort until one has experimented with them, and the experiment is well worth trying.

Live Foods

The majority of seed-eating birds also eat some insects, but it is rarely possible to provide for them in captivity those insects which they are accustomed to find for themselves in the wild. Nevertheless, there are a number of substitutes available which can be used to advantage. Probably the best live food of all is ant cocoons. Unfortunately, to collect these in any quantity requires a good deal of skill as well as plenty of spare time. For those who live in the country it is not at all difficult to find an ant's nest. A spadeful of the nest put in a tin and later emptied out on the floor of the aviary will usually not only provide live ant cocoons but also live ants which will be snapped up by many species and be considered a great treat.

Greenfly, which often infest rose bushes, will be eaten by a number of the smaller species, but naturally if insecticides have been used on the bushes, the greenfly are suspect and should not be used.

There is also a very small fly known

Food and Water

as the fruit fly (*Drosophila*) which is much appreciated by many very small birds. These fruit flies can be bred quite simply in a mixture of bran and banana in a jar, but it is rather more difficult to feed them to the birds unless they have been taught by experience to extract these flies through the cork in a small glass container. Nectar-feeding birds, with their long beaks, have no difficulty at all in putting the beak through such a cork into a small tube in which the flies have been placed, and then licking up the flies with their long tongues, but seed eaters are short-billed and cannot achieve the same success. However, if fruit flies can be obtained, they are worth feeding.

An excellent live food for the larger birds, those species which are larger than the small waxbills, are gentles, which can be procured comparatively cheaply from firms which breed them. They are really bred for anglers, but the bird keeper can also use them to his birds' advantage. They are excellent food, in the form of both the larva and the pupa. By the time the pupa turns into a blowfly, it can probably only be tackled by the larger birds which are quick on the wing and can also deal with a fly of this size.

One of the great assets of gentles is that birds seem to come to no harm however many of them they eat, and thus, for the person who is unable to obtain other forms of live food, the gentle is a real standby.

Probably the most common of all live foods which can be readily purchased is the mealworm, but this worm has its dangers, for too many mealworms produce liver troubles. Because of this fact mealworms should be strictly rationed. If only a few birds are kept, a quarter of a pound of mealworms will last quite a long time, provided that they are kept in a ventilated tin in which there is several inches of bran. It is a mistake to buy too many mealworms at one time because they too pupate and the pupae turn into beetles. These beetles lay eggs which hatch into worms, but the breeding cycle is so long that for the majority of bird keepers who want mealworms it is not worthwhile trying to breed them at home. If the bird keeper wants to breed his own mealworms, it can be done by having a container the size of a biscuit tin with holes in the top for ventilation and bran as the medium for them to live in. The addition of some vegetable such as carrot or spinach leaves supplies the necessary moisture which the bettles require. After these preparations so much patience is necessary that the average fancier finds that a quarter of a pound of mealworms bought from time to time is a small expense that saves a lot of trouble.

During the summer there are a number of small caterpillars which can be found in the garden, and some of these are useful for bird feeding. Hairy varieties should not be fed, and it is only really safe to feed the small green caterpillars which are often so abundant.

Food and Water

There are others which are quite useful as an addition to diet, but unless the bird owner knows something about caterpillars, he should confine his attention to those which are green, hairless and small.

Houseflies, too, are eaten readily by some species, and are a very valuable form of food, but one has to be careful to see that they have not been in contact with either flypapers or cards which have been impregnated with insecticide. Thus, it is usually unwise to feed flies which are already dead. Those which are caught in a room free from possible contamination, and killed at once, are quickly picked up by many species of exotic finches.

It must be added here, however, that not all birds are interested in live food. For them one must try to think out other means of supplying what may be lacking in their unnatural diet if they cannot be persuaded to eat insects of any sort. The task is not a difficult one, but it does require some thought.

Additions to Diet

Insectile mixtures which are prepared for softbills are often eaten quite readily by seed eaters as well, particularly if they are kept with birds for which this food is a normal diet. Insectile mixtures which contain a variety of ingredients, including flesh foods, can make up for the deficiencies mentioned in the last section when referring to those birds which will not take live foods.

Another valuable addition to diet for birds which are not kept in direct daylight and who get no actual sunshine at all is cod-liver oil. This is particularly valuable for birds which are kept in a cage in a living room all the year round and for those birds in an outside aviary whose flying in the open air has to be strictly limited during the winter months. The best way to feed cod-liver oil is to impregnate seed with it. This is quite a simple process. A pound jar of seed has carefully poured over the top of it a full teaspoonful of cod-liver oil. The jar is allowed to stand while the oil gradually percolates through the seed to the bottom. The best thing to do then is to remove the seed at the top, which will not be found to be too sticky, and to put it straight into the feeding pots. Seed which has been treated in this way can be fed throughout the winter if not more than one teaspoonful is used for each pound of seed. Naturally much of the oil will be wasted because the birds described in this book hardly eat any of the husk by intention, but they will get some of the cod-liver oil which will not only have got onto the husk, but will have found its way through into the kernel as well.

It is just possible that providing vitamin D in this way may make it necessary to increase the amount of vitamin E that the birds have in their diet. This need not be a serious problem, for there are a number of suitable vitamin mixtures on the market

Food and Water

which can be fed to the birds to make sure that all their vitamin needs are supplied. A very suitable compound is ABDEC, and one drop of this added to a water pot such as is used in a Budgerigar cage is adequate if given twice a week. There is such a thing as vitamin poisoning, and it is thus a mistake to think that such compounds should be given every day. Twice a week is adequate, and will produce no ill effects, but may be very beneficial to the birds.

One other food ought to be mentioned here as an addition to diet, and that is the egg food which is so well known to the canary breeder. This food is very much appreciated by quite a number of exotic birds which are seed eaters, and they will often eat it in considerable quantity when they have young in the nest.

Digestion

The digestion of a bird is a very complicated business, but this subject cannot be dealt with fully here. What must be said is that a bird has no teeth, and therefore it requires assistance in grinding up its food. This can be catered for by the provision of sand and grit and powdered oyster or cockle shell. Probably the best way to supply the grinding tools for seed eaters is to buy mineralized grit. This will carry out the mechanical job of crushing the seed in the gizzard and will also, because some

of it is absorbed, provide the birds with some of the essential minerals which they require. Mineralized grits are cheap, and are probably better than anything one is likely to be able to provide by making up one's own mixtures at home.

Just one word of warning is needed on the subject of grit. It is that those birds which have not been using it for some time should be limited rigorously in quantity. Now that birds come from abroad by air more often than by sea, grit is usually only withheld from them for a matter of a few days; perhaps even so, it is still advisable to ration them for the first few days. Grit when eaten to excess finds its way into the intestines and sets up serious irritation.

Cuttlebone, either in powdered form or as the actual skeleton of the squid, should always be available. Birds like cuttlebone, and apparently the calcium it contains is readily absorbed by them. The great thing to bear in mind with regard to cuttlebone, however, is that what is found on the seashore has to be thoroughly cleaned before it is given to any birds. Cuttlebone not only contains calcium, but it also contains salt which is valuable in moderate quantity.

It is obvious, of course, that this chapter does not contain all that can be said on the subject of feeding exotic seed eaters, but in the sections dealing with the individual species the question of their particular diet has usually been referred to with some care.

General Management

It is most important with all livestock hobbies that they should be a pleasure and never be allowed to become a burden, for if that does happen, the beginner soon grows tired and gives up what might have provided him with countless hours of pleasure for many years ahead.

The cleaning of cages and shelters is a matter which has to be dealt with regularly. It is useless to allow cages to become really dirty, and then, only when one feels that they are a disgrace, to set about the task of cleaning. The sensible thing to do is to have regular days for cleaning, and for most fanciers the weekend is the most suitable time. The frequency with which cleaning is carried out will depend, to some extent, upon the owner's sparse time, but as a general rule, the more frequently cages and flights can be cleaned, the better. One of the first rules for satisfactory bird keeping is to provide clean and therefore hygienic accommodation for the birds.

Lighting

Generally speaking, birds do not need artificial light, but for the bird owner it is a great advantage to have his rooms and shelters equipped with adequate lighting, otherwise in the winter he will not be able to spend much time, if any, with his birds in the evenings. The simplest form of lighting is electric, but there are alternatives. These alternatives may be cheaper, but on the other hand, they may be more dangerous. Where electric light is used and the birds are in full light at times when it is dark outside, it is more or less essential to have a dimmer fitted to the circuit. It alarms birds if they are suddenly plunged from full light into darkness. It often scares them so much that if they are not on the perches at the time when the light is put out, they immediately fly up to the top of the cage and may do considerable damage to themselves.

There are a number of dimmers advertised in the fancy press, and these are easy to fit. When they have been set, it is possible to reduce the light gradually so that the birds have an opportunity of settling themselves for the night without any feeling of panic.

Artificial Heat

Few of the birds which are described in this book require artificial heat in winter, but many of them are, nevertheless, all the better for it. From the point of view of the owner, the ability to heat his shelter or bird room is extremely valuable. There is no fun at all in working with birds when the temperature is below freezing and one is compelled to wear overcoat and gloves to do what is necessary. There can be no pleasure in the task under such conditions.

Many of the birds which come from tropical countries are quite used to low temperatures at night, and there is no need to keep the temperature of either bird room or shelter above 55 to 60 F. with seed eaters.

Sometimes the bird owner gets the idea that he should keep his birds in a constant temperature. That idea is entirely wrong and, if carried into practice, is certainly not good for the birds. In a state of nature they are quite accustomed to very considerable variation between the temperature of day and night, and they are probably fitter and generally hardier because of it. They have their own means of insulation against cold, for with their feathers puffed out they produce excellent insulation against outside cold, and thus preserve their body heat.

Disease and Accident

However careful the bird owner may be, sooner or later he will experience disease among his stock, or it may be that some birds will become the victims of accident. For such contingencies as these he must be prepared. It would be quite wrong, however, to create the impression that disease is one of those misfortunes which is bound to strike seriously at some time or another and that there is nothing that can be done to prevent it. The extent of the seriousness of disease among birds kept in captivity always depends to a very large degree on the care which is bestowed upon the birds.

The most important thing always is prevention, and in many ways it is easier to pevent disease than it is to cure it. Birds are always difficult patients, and the amount of research which has been carried out with regard to the illnesses of birds is so small that the remedies one is compelled to employ become very largely empiric. What one man finds useful for his birds under certain conditions another finds quite useless.

Perhaps the greatest asset any bird keeper can have is the ability to notice that a bird is unwell before it is, in fact, seriously ill. This "stock sense" which some people possess to a very high degree is of the utmost value. On the other hand, there are some bird keepers who do not realize that their birds are ill until they are almost at the point of death. When that stage is reached, the hopes of recovery must be extremely small.

Every day individual birds should be looked at, and any changes in appearance must be recognized. One of the best ways to prevent disease, of course, is strict cleanliness in cages, bird room, and aviary. The more the birds are allowed to clean themselves and the more frequently the cages are cleaned, the less likelihood there is of trouble, particularly when it is an isolated bird which suddenly develops a disease which is later found to be infectious.

Newly imported birds are always a danger because one never knows what infection they may have been in contact with; so to prevent trouble, birds which are purchased, even from breeders in this country, should always be isolated for a time, perhaps for as long as two or three weeks, before they are put in with birds which are known to be fit. This statement has already been made in an earlier section of the book, but it is so important that repetition here is not a mere waste of space.

Signs of Disease

As has already been suggested, the bird keeper should look to see if his birds appear fit. The bird which sits with its eyes closed is obviously unwell and should immediately be separated from the others. Any bird which is off its food is usually a sick bird, for as a rule, seed eaters are almost continuous feeders. A bird which sits with its feathers all fluffed up is feeling the cold, probably because it has not been feeding and has thus been unable to maintain its body heat. It can reasonably be inferred from human experience that illness and feeling chilled often go together.

The breathing of birds is hardly ever noticed when they are fit, but any bird that is sick may breathe with an irregular rhythm. It may also breathe noisily as well. Birds in this condition may be suffering from any of a variety of diseases, but it is essential that they should be put on their own so that some treatment can be attempted.

Perhaps the best general remedy for the ills of birds is heat, and if a cure is possible—it must be remembered that some diseases are quite incurable—a high temperature will help to get the bird into that state where it will start to feed again. The temperature must be really high to be useful, and anything from 85 to 90 F. is the lowest range that can be considered satisfactory. If the bird is put in a lower temperature, one might just as well save oneself the trouble of producing artificial heat at all.

The best way of providing a bird with a temperature of this order is to place it in a hospital cage. There can be no doubt whatever that one of the most valuable pieces of equipment that any bird fancier can ever have is a hospital cage, for it is an investment which will repay its cost many times over a period of a few years.

The idea of the hospital cage is perfectly simple. It is usually a smaller cage than that to which the bird is accustomed. It is constructed with a false bottom under which there is some means of heating, usually electric light bulbs. The heat in the hospital cage must be controlled by a thermostat, and these instruments are so accurate today that it is possible to maintain the temperature in a hospital cage to within 2 or 3 F. of what is considered to be the best temperature for effecting a cure. During illness a constant temperature, as well as a high one, is important.

Breeding

Although there are many thousands of bird fanciers in this country, both men and women, who are keenly interested in keeping exotic finches, probably only a comparatively small proportion of them are interested in breeding these birds. Many find that their pleasure is complete if they have a number of colorful and interesting birds in a cage in the living room. However, there are many hundreds of others for whom the breeding of the exotic birds which they keep as a hobby is a matter of the greatest interest, and year by year species are added to the list of those which, up to that moment, have not previously been bred successfully in captivity. The keeping of finches is a world-wide hobby, which means that there are many thousands who eventually become breeders and are prepared to share their experiences with other fanciers.

Despite the large number of years over which exotic birds have been kept as pets, there are still many species which have defied all the skill and wiles of the would-be breeder. This fact provides a fascination of its own, and year by year some fanciers continue to try to breed a species with which all who have kept it in the past have failed.

In general, the successful breeding of finches depends upon a number of factors, but these can be summed up by the expression "the right environment." Unless birds which come from foreign countries can find in captivity here conditions which remind them fairly nearly of the environment to which they have been accustomed, the chances are that they will not attempt to breed. Thus, the art of successful breeding depends to a very large extent upon the observation and deduction of the person who is keeping birds and who hopes that he can persuade them to breed. These fanciers have so to change conditions when they are unsuccessful that these alterations in themselves seem to make it more probable that the birds will feel at home and ready to start to produce a family. This may sound quite simple, but in fact it is by no means easy to realize what any particular species needs. Even when one feels that these needs have been understood, it is often very difficult to cater to them in practice.

Breeding Age

Not all birds breed at the same age, and it is, of course, quite probable that the inexperienced fancier will try to get birds to go to nest when they are still immature. If failure follows, he may be surprised, but sooner or later he will realize what was wrong. The man of experience can usually tell from the appearance of his birds whether they are sufficiently mature to be ready for breeding or not.

In a book of this sort there is no need to be too scientific, but the fact remains that one must realize that the age of maturity in different species may vary from as little as four months to two years or even more. The birds dealt with here should breed in the year following that in which they were born, but there are some species which are remarkably precocious.

Birds are unlikely to breed unless they are thoroughly fit, and this is a state which cannot be achieved in a matter of a few days. The conditioning of birds may well extend over a period of months, and very often the way in which these birds have been treated during the preceding winter decides whether they will breed or not the following spring.

There are a number of factors which must be borne in mind when one is attempting to condition birds for breeding. Perhaps there are three things which are of the greatest importance in this respect. The first is good feeding; the second is plenty of fresh air with as much sunlight as possible, which means direct sunlight and not light received through ordinary window glass; and thirdly, exercise. It is more than foolish to house birds during the winter in quarters in which there is insufficient room for them to take adequate exercise, and particularly is this the case with regard to hens which, if they are not allowed freedom of flight during the winter, may lose muscle tone, and then, later, when they attempt to breed early the next year, are more likely than not to suffer from egg binding.

There is another point too which is of interest. In a state of nature not all species keep together in pairs throughout the year. It is quite common with some of them to separate into groups, either groups of mixed sexes or groups of cocks or hens, in the out-of-breeding season. That is a fact which is worth remembering with birds that are kept in captivity, for it often happens that a pair of birds which are kept together during the winter are less interested in breeding than those which have been separated during the off-season. With some species it is almost impossible to keep cocks and hens together except during the breeding season, for the cocks sometimes become extremely spiteful, and so harass the hens that they can never get into breeding condition, even if they are able to remain relatively unharmed.

"True" Pairs

The sexes are so much alike in some species that it is only the real expert who is able to distinguish them easily by any physical characteristics. The result of this fact is that the only true test of sex is behavior. This may be annoying, but it is a fact which the fancier has to face, and before he is able to find a "true" pair he may have to put several "pairs" together, so that, after careful observation, he may become convinced that at last he has found at least one cock and hen among his segregated couples.

Birds are sometimes amusing,

Breeding

although perhaps also exasperating, in that two hens may act as though they were a pair with the only result that there is a nest full of eggs, all of which are infertile. Even two cocks can flatter only to deceive by setting to work to build a nest and then going no further with the cycle, for the simple reason that nest building is the limit of their capacity. Very often it is cheaper and a saving of time for the fancier who wishes to breed a particular species to purchase a pair which have already bred together. The initial cost may be greater, but in the long run, the extra expense may be well worthwhile.

The Desire to Breed

When a pair has been obtained, it is usually the cock who gives the first indication of a desire to breed. He will pay considerable attention to the hen. He may feed her, and in the case of very many species the cock will display before the hen to give her due warning of his desires and intentions. This courting display, which varies quite considerably between one genus and another, is often amusing to watch, and is always a source of fascination to the bird keeper, who is inevitably optimistic when he sees these signs. He can always see in his imagination that within a few weeks there will be young in the nest. That he is frequently disappointed is no serious discouragement, for he has to be an optimist.

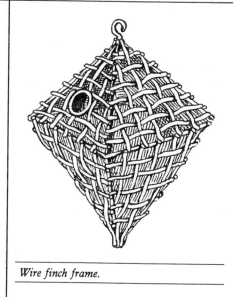

Wire finch frame.

Breeding Quarters

As has already been stated, unless the environment provided for the birds is suitable, few species will make any attempt to breed at all. It is thus essential that considerable thought should be given to the question of breeding quarters.

Many species which show no inclination to breed in a cage immediately become interested when they are placed in an aviary. Such an aviary need not be large, for a structure with a flight 6 ft. long is ample for many of the smaller species. However, there are many other species which will not breed in an aviary unless it is one which has been carefully provided with plants and bushes. For some of them to

40

Breeding

gain that confidence which is essential for successful breeding, there must be not only bushes but also climbing plants in profusion in which they can conceal both themselves and their nests. One can only learn what the birds need from experience, and if a particular pair, which belongs to a species which has already been bred in captivity with comparative ease, shows no wish to breed in an outside aviary, then it may be that the addition of plants will cause them to alter their minds and to set to work on nest building straight away.

Nesting Receptacles

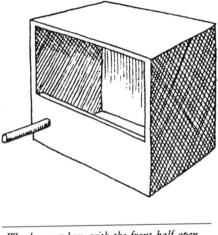

Wooden nest box, with the front half open.

There are a number of nesting receptacles which can be provided, and it is a good idea to see that there is a variety of such nests placed in the aviary so that the birds can have a free choice. Some species are more likely to nest in a wooden box, others prefer a wire finch frame, while there are species which are interested in neither of these but will immediately start to nest if somewhere in the aviary there is hung up a clump of gorse or heather. There are, too, those birds which always insist on building in a bush.

It would be unwise to suggest that particular species are addicted to particular types of receptacles, for the simple reason that one often finds that one pair of a certain species chooses a box while another prefers the wire finch frame. Thus, by far the best thing to do

is to provide more different nesting sites than there are pairs of birds.

It quite often happens that a pair of birds which has been provided with all the different types of nesting site enumerated here still shows no inclination to build a nest of its own. Sometimes this pair can be persuaded to do something constructive if a nest is partially built for them in a box or wire frame.

In a small aviary it is probably wiser to try to breed with only one pair, because during the breeding season birds are quarrelsome creatures. Unless there is ample space, they are likely to interfere with each other, and then perhaps all of them give up the effort of raising a family.

Even so, this statement still requires

Breeding

some modification, for there are species which seem to breed much better when several pairs are housed together in the same enclosure. When the fancier has read the species accounts, he will have the necessary information which will allow him to make preparations likely to produce the success he hopes for.

The Golden Rule

There is one rule which is of inestimable value to all bird fanciers who are interested in breeding exotics. It is that once breeding has started, the birds should not be interfered with at all. The temptation to look into the nest to see if the first egg has been laid may be very great, but it is a temptation which must be resisted, for the majority of species resent interference while their breeding operations are in progress. If they are disturbed, they are very likely to desert. It is far better to wait and find out by observation whether eggs have been laid and, later, whether chicks have been hatched. By standing well away from the site of the nest, one can usually tell whether the hen is sitting. If she disappears for long periods, the signs are good, for it is unlikely that she has died.

There can be no doubt at all that there have been more failures in the breeding of exotic birds through the interference of the owner than from any other cause, even with those species which are reasonably free breeders.

Chicks in the Nest

If one is observant, it is often comparatively easy to know when the eggs have hatched, for at that time the normal thing is for both parents to be most assiduous in collecting food to take to their young, and the number of journeys they make to and from the nest will be much greater than at normal times. Some chicks give evidence of their existence by the noise they make even a few days after they have been hatched, but others remain completely silent almost until the day when they emerge from the nest as fledglings.

There are a number of species in which the adult birds eat seed almost entirely and for the greater part of the year are comparatively uninterested in live foods; yet when they have young in the nest, they are most anxious to find live foods to feed to the chicks. If they cannot find this food, the young may quickly die of starvation.

In the sections dealing with individual species it will be stated in most cases whether the young are fed almost entirely on live food, so that the fancier can make preparations in good time. It is always extremely difficult to cater to such birds, particularly if they are small ones, because the type of live food required must also necessarily be small and is very often difficult to obtain. It is almost certain that unless the young receive the food which is natural to them, they will not live, for there is nothing that the parents can do to

Breeding

satisfy them from the limited space even of a planted aviary.

The easiest birds to cater to are those which feed their young entirely on seed. It may be seed which has been taken into their own crops and is regurgitated after being partially digested, or it may merely be seed which has been husked and is fed almost in its natural state.

The Fledglings

The time that the young spend in the nest after being hatched varies very considerably from species to species. It may be as short as ten days, it may be as long as twenty-one. The longer the birds are in the nest, the nearer they are to being independent when they emerge; but most young birds need still to be fed by their parents after they have come out of the nest, and suitable food must be provided for them at this time. It will be noticed that the young quite quickly attempt to feed themselves on the diet which will be natural to them when they are adult, but they will also rely upon what is given to them by their parents.

Sometimes the cock is difficult between the time when the young leave the nest and the age when they can fend for themselves. He may have fed the young birds extremely well while they were in the nest, but when they are outside he seems to be anxious for the hen to start to breed again, and he may not only refuse to feed the young, but he may even be rough with them. If he is seen to be spiteful, the cock must be removed, and the burden of feeding has to be left to the hen—a task which she is quite capable of performing unaided in normal circumstances. If a further nest is required, just as soon as the young are fully independent, they can be removed to a separate compartment, and the cock can then be brought back to the hen.

Growing to Maturity

It often happens that chicks leave the nest, are fed by their parents until they can fend for themselves without any assistance, and then begin to develop satisfactorily but do not survive until the following spring. Many attempts have been made to explain why this happens, but none of the explanations carries complete conviction. It is probable, of course, that during the period they were in the nest their feeding was inadequate, and that this fact has made them less robust for when they are separated and put on their own. Perhaps too little is known of the requirements of young birds between the age when they are separated from their parents and the time when they themselves become fully adult, but as the years go by and the hobby of finch breeding increases in scope, many of the questions which are now unanswered will be satisfactorily solved.

Waxbills

A ll the species treated in the following pages belong to the family of estrildid finches, the Estrildidae. The name *waxbill* has been used to refer to the entire family, but *waxbill* more particularly has been given to a large number of small birds which come chiefly from the African continent. Most of these birds have a beak which looks like a piece of red sealing wax, but there are one or two exceptions that do not fit into the scheme. Thus, the term *waxbill* must be regarded as a popular name without any real scientific significance.

Orange-cheeked Waxbill (*Estrilda melpoda*). The Orange-cheeked Waxbill, although none of its colors is really bright, is an extremely beautiful little bird, showing, as it does, delicate shades of gray, brown, red, and yellow. When it is in really first-class condition, there is never a feather out of place and it looks a picture of graceful contour. Its activity and antics in an aviary are as amusing as those of the members of the tit family, and it is justly popular as either a cage or an aviary bird.

It needs some care when it is first imported, although it will usually take readily to small yellow millet, with the result that it can soon be persuaded to feed, which is the first step with newly imported exotics. Once acclimated it is very hardy and can endure a wide variation in temperature, but like most birds, it can die very quickly if treated with too little care at any time. There is no reason why it should not be kept outdoors all the year round if precautions are taken to protect it from cold winds and it also has a dry place in which to roost. In a northerly climate a wooden finch box with a handful of soft hay inside will provide an ideal roosting place for the winter. Naturally the nest box will be in the shelter and not in the flight.

Although there are certain variations in color which should be looked for when a pair is being chosen, it has to be admitted that selection for sex is rarely an easy matter. It may not be difficult to choose a few birds that seem obviously to be cocks, but from a large consignment there are very few indeed which can easily be recognized, although later it may be found that the sexes were fairly evenly divided in the consignment.

The distinctive characteristic of this species is the orange-yellow patch on the cheeks. Some birds have a larger patch than others, but it is not safe to assume that all birds with the largest patches are cocks. The density of the color in the patch varies considerably during the course of the year, and if memory is good, it will probably be found that those birds which have developed the brightest cheek patches when in full color are, in fact, cocks. Unfortunately, condition is something which is not constant, and all birds are not at their best at the same time of the year, so the average breeder can be excused if he fails to pick out a pair.

Breeding Orange-cheeked Waxbills is

no easy matter, but it has been achieved even in a cage. Thus, it is all the more surprising that so few pairs attempt to build a nest even when their environment seems ideal, when they are housed in a well-planted aviary. There have been a number of reports of nests being build in bushes, in nest boxes and even in wire finch frames, a catholicity of taste which is of little help to the breeder. There has even been a record of two hens building a nest and sitting quite hopefully on the eggs, but accounts of successful rearing are comparatively few. There have been pairs which have bred on more than one occasion, while others have built a nest and even incubated the eggs in their first year of captivity, and from that time have never made a similar attempt, although they remained fit and lived happily in confinement for a number of years. Thus, the bird lover who wishes to breed the Orange-cheeked Waxbill must be prepared for many disappointments, for they will certainly come.

Nest building is a casual business, as this little bird seems content with the flimsiest of structures and rarely takes the trouble even to line the nest. When the hen has laid, both birds will incubate the eggs, although the hen does most of the sitting. The cock is usually content to sit beside her in the nest, perhaps just to show that he is on guard.

A number of records of hatchings have been reported, but so often these accounts have ended on a tragic note, for the parents have, for some unknown reason, ceased to feed their young after the first few days. Probably the reason for this neglect is that the adults are unable to find the live food they expect for feeding their young. The conclusion to draw from this is that the chances of success are greater when a large variety of small insect life can be provided. It may not be impossible, but it is certainly difficult, for the breeder to achieve this variety at any time of the year, and he can only hope that a large, planted aviary will supply a sufficiency.

The young, when they leave the nest, are dull-colored birds with all the grays and browns of the adults so arranged that the top of the body is brown while underneath it is an unrelieved gray with no hint of orange or yellow. The beak is a very dark gray. Adult plumage is assumed at the first molt, and it is at this time that the beak also changes to a bright red.

Feeding adults is not difficult, but the taste of the Orange-cheeked Waxbill seems very limited. The main article of diet is small yellow millet, and some birds will not even attempt to husk white millet or even small canary. Nevertheless, a small quantity of white millet and canary should always be available. Millet sprays are a favorite food, and these little birds seem happy to stand on their heads and flutter their tails as they pick the seeds from the spray. Seeding grasses are always popular and should be provided whenever they are available.

As these Orange-cheeked Waxbills spend a considerable part of their time on the ground scratching over and picking at the soil in search of food, it would be more than useful if one knew what they were really trying to find. It may be that they are searching for small insects, or perhaps it is for seed which has germinated in the soil. To provide the insects for which they are looking may be impossible in many areas, but sprouted seeds are easily prepared and should be given to the birds frequently.

Red-eared Waxbill (Black-rumped Waxbill, *Estrilda troglodytes*). One of the great advantages of this small bird for the beginner is that it has always been imported in large numbers, and is consequently cheap. If properly treated, it is hardy enough and soon becomes a very active inmate of either cage or aviary. It has one disadvantage, however, from the point of view of the bird keeper who likes to get on reasonably friendly terms with his birds, for the Red-eared Waxbill rarely shows any desire to become tame in the smallest degree, and does not often take any apparent interest in humans except to regard them with suspicion. There are always exceptions, and much depends upon the care and trouble which the bird keeper takes in an endeavor to win the confidence of his birds. As a group the seed eaters are disinclined even to feed when their owner is near the food pots.

This species has been bred in captivity both purely and also by crossing with several other species of waxbill, but it would definitely be a mistake to think that it is easy to breed, for the exact opposite is, in fact, the case. Some pairs will build a nest and lay eggs, and then discontinue their domestic activities, but more often than not the pair will show not the slightest inclination to breed at any time. An interesting feature about the nest is the special shelter which the cock often builds for himself on top. There he is quite prepared to spend the night while the hen is sitting.

One difficulty, and probably it is only one of many, is that the sexes are by no means easy to distinguish, and thus the finding of a true pair presents a considerable problem. It is said that the width of the eye streak is slightly narrower in the hen, but this seems such a subtle distinction that it is rarely helpful. Dealers are by no means prepared to stake their reputations on selecting pairs by this method.

Some enthusiastic and observant owners of this species have noticed that the intensity of the pink suffusion apparent on the belly is also an indication of sex. It is true that birds which are very brightly colored in this area are almost certainly cocks, but the time of year and the age of the birds complicates the issue, and the fact still remains that true pairs are difficult to select.

Feeding is a simple matter, for, if the birds are left to choose for themselves, the Red-eared Waxbill will show a preference for small yellow millet. If white millet and canary are also available, some of these seeds will be eaten, but canary seems to present a problem to this small bird when it tries to remove the husk, and rather surprisingly it finds white millet easier to manage. Millet sprays are rather expensive, but they should be provided, and the antics of the little Red-eared Waxbill on a suspended millet spray are ample reward for a little extra expense.

Green food is pecked at rather than eaten, but seeding grasses are a favorite food and should be given whenever they can be obtained. Even suspended sprays of seeding weeds will not only attract the attention of the birds, but they will also find something to eat in such a clump.

Although the Red-eared Waxbill shows comparatively little interest in the conventional live foods which the bird owner can buy, it enjoys catching gnats and other small flies on the wing, and will dart out from its hiding place to pounce upon this type of live food which is frequently present in the flight on summer evenings.

Red Avadavat (Strawberry Finch, *Amandava amandava*). The Red Avadavat certainly possesses one remarkable difference to distinguish it from all the other waxbills. It is that the cock of this species adopts a nuptial plumage for the breeding season, and then, later on in the year, loses his bright colors to become almost as drab as his mate. Unfortunately, when the next breeding season comes round, in captivity not all cocks attain to the same brightness of plumage which they normally display in the wild. With most species which show red in the plumage, there is a tendency for the brightness of this color to be lost progressively after each molt in captivity, but there are several notable exceptions among the estrildid finches.

The cock, when in nuptial plumage, is a very dark red-brown on the back. The tail is black, but the coverts show a distinct bronze sheen. The rest of the body is a bright red, but well spotted with white. The extent of this spotting may also be indicative of a local variation, but probably no one has bothered to go closely into the matter of these spots. The beak, as in nearly all the waxbills, is red, and the brilliance of its color, as so often happens, is an indication of condition. The hen is much more sombrely clad, for she is really a gray bird, darker on top, where the gray is clearly tinged with brown, and a paler gray underneath usually tinted there with yellow, although some hens show even a shade of pink on the underside. The Red Avadavat is a small bird slightly less than 4 in. in length.

One of their virtues is that they are reasonably hardy and can be kept outdoors all the year round, although it is safer to keep imported birds in a slightly warmed shelter during the winter. Young birds bred in aviaries are able to endure without harm even the worst winter weather with its combination of frost, snow, and even fog.

Many aviculturists have tried to breed this little bird in a cage, but success under such conditions is almost impossible. The Red Avadavat will breed in an aviary, but it is not too easy, as many will know who have tried without success. There have been a number of breeders who have been most successful, even going so far as to breed several generations down from imported stock. The story of their successes is an incentive even if those who try to emulate them do not achieve immediate success themselves.

The best chances of successful breeding occur when there is a considerable variety of nesting sites which can be chosen by the birds at will. Nest boxes and wire finch frames should be hung up, but as these are by no means natural sites for the nests, tall grass and bushes should also be available. In the wild they are much more accustomed to building their nests near the ground than in either tall bushes or trees.

It is not unusual for the Red Avadavat to build a nest, and for the hen to follow this activity by the laying of a full clutch. But, so often, the attempt to start a family then ends with no apparent reason for this abandonment of their domestic duties.

Normally the adults seem to be interested in only white and yellow millet, but some are very partial to sprouted canary even if they will not look at it in its dormant state. Nevertheless, the seed mixture should contain a small amount of canary as well as an addition of weed seeds, which are always picked over with keen curiosity if not actual relish.

The Red Avadavat needs small insects in abundance if a family is to be reared, but some of these birds show little interest in such food at any other time. Even if the Red Avadavat is conservative in its likes and dislikes, every attempt should be made to interest it in as wide a variety of foods as possible.

In an aviary containing a mixed collection of small birds, the Red Avadavat is peaceful, but it will not tolerate the close proximity of its own kind if it makes up its mind to start breeding. The interference of any other species at this time is resented, and the intruder is driven away with much fury and little ceremony, but no harm is done. Actually the fierceness of this avadavat is more amusing to the owner than dangerous to any of the other birds.

The brightness of the nuptial plumage of the cock, when coupled with the general curiosity and constant activity of a pair, makes the Red Avadavat a very popular aviary bird. The cock even tries to sing, but the merit of his effort seems to lie very largely in the ear of the owner who keeps him. Perhaps the best that can be said is that his song is pleasant and never harsh, and it is an interesting vocal effort to himself and his mate, for whom it is really intended.

Waxbills

Red-cheeked Cordonbleu

(Uraeginthus bengalus). Although this little cordonbleu—and it is small, for it is no more than 3 in. long, including its medium-sized tail—is an extremely popular waxbill, and by comparison cheap, it is inclined to be a disappointment when first purchased by the novice enthusiast. The reason for this disappointment is that newly imported birds frequently die within a few weeks because those who receive them do not know how to acclimate them safely. It is a fact that these birds are definitely delicate when they first come into the country, and need particular care, but they can be managed. If they are not handled well during these first few critical weeks, they will either die, or if they survive will rarely become even reasonably hardy.

Two things are essential for satisfactory acclimation: the right temperature and correct feeding. There will be very few losses indeed if the temperature of their cage can be regulated within narrow limits. For the first fortnight a temperature of around 65 F. is just right, and then by gradual stages it can be reduced to 55 F. over a period of four weeks. It will thus be quite obvious that the most convenient time to acquire Red-cheeked Cordonbleus is in the late spring when the maintenance of the temperatures suggested will not be difficult. Importations are made quite frequently, and there is no need to buy newly imported birds in the middle of winter. Drafts are lethal for the Red-cheeked Cordonbleu, and damp will produce a fatal pneumonia in no time. Thus, the birds should first be kept in a box-type cage in a well-lighted room.

It is often of considerable advantage to put these cordonbleus in with other small birds which have learned to eat an insectile mixture, for frequently they will imitate their companions, and no one who has kept these birds will deny the value of a high-quality insectile mixture to get them really fit. Live food is also of great value, and ants, if not live ant cocoons, are usually obtainable without much difficulty. *Drosophila* are an ideal food, and are easily bred, but it is not an easy matter to provide them in adequate quantities nor to keep them in the cage long enough for them to be caught and eaten. Some fanciers put their *Drosophila*, or fruit flies, in small glass tubes with a hole in the cork, and some waxbills will wait by the cork for the flies to emerge.

As breeders Red-cheeked Cordonbleus are unreliable, but one does sometimes come across a pair which are prolific and at the same time ideal parents. Very many pairs will build a nest, and they seem not to mind whether they use a nest box or a wire finch nest for the purpose. The nest itself is carefully built from grass and small roots, but is lined almost casually with any feathers that happen to be available.

The preliminary to building the nest is the courtship display of the male, which is characteristic of the display of most waxbills, but differs in one particular. The dance on the perch with a piece of grass in the beak is definitely characteristic of most of the cocks of this genus, but the male Red-cheek adds to this the dropping of his wings as he hops up and down in front of the hen.

The eggs are small and white, and the average number for a clutch is four, but there have been quite a number of reports of as many as seven eggs being laid in the nest. Although both birds busy themselves with the building of the nest, practically all the incubating is done by the hen. Some cocks never seem to sit on the eggs at all, but merely take up a defensive attitude on the box when the hen comes off for a little exercise.

Generally speaking, Red-cheeked Cordonbleus are very inoffensive little birds, but during the breeding season cocks are inclined to be short tempered with inquisitive companions. Both birds are really rather apprehensive at this time, and if they are interfered with will forsake the nest, but before they abandon their home they try to drive off intruders.

Incubation takes roughly thirteen days, but as the birds are so easily scared, those who have bred them successfully are not too anxious to pry into these details more than is absolutely necessary. From the time the chicks hatch it is quite obvious that a family is being reared, for both birds are constantly searching for small insect life which is rarely available in sufficient quantities in the aviary. The breeder has to do the best he can, and if worse comes to worst, minced insect food must be provided if the insects available are too large for the birds to manage. It is probable that in a wild state the only food provided for the young in the nest is live food which has, however, been partially predigested by the parents.

The time that the young remain in the nest varies quite considerably, but is never less than fourteen days and may even extend to eighteen. Perhaps it is unwise to be dogmatic, and one should only say that it seems likely that the longer the youngsters remain in the nest, the greater is their chance of survival. Even when they are well feathered and out of the nest, the young are still fed by the parents for at least a week and sometimes for ten days.

As has been said already, the Red-cheeked Cordonbleu is an unrealiable breeder, although there are a number of records to show that it has even hybridized with several other species which are closely related to it.

These birds live almost entirely on small yellow millet and spray millet, and are not inclined to take much interest in any other seeds. Their taste in green food is definitely selective, and the widest variety of seeding grasses should be provided so that they can make their own choice. They will soon show their preference, but no two birds seem to have exactly the same taste.

Finches

This chapter includes two of the major groups of estrildid finches: the grass-finches and the parrot-finches.

A few of these finches can be bred in an ordinary box cage, while others will breed with greater success in an aviary, but it must not be thought that all are free breeders in captivity.

In these groups of exotics are some of the most beautifully colored birds in the world, and side by side with them will be found other birds which, although modest in appearance, have other attractions for the aviculturist. Thus, for those who want color in their birds, here they will find species which are bound to please, and for those who prefer beauty of form, some of these finches will certainly satisfy their desire. The bird lover who cannot find in this group some species which he would like to keep must indeed be hard to please.

Zebra Finch *(Poephila guttata).* The Zebra Finch is a most remarkable little bird which came originally from Australia, but which has now almost become a domesticated species not only in this country but also in others.

Right from the start this little bird was popular, for it was always active and showed no fear either of man or of other species of exotic birds of which it could not possibly have had any experience. One of its great virtues was that it was so easy to acclimate, and very few birds were lost during the time they were housed in a cage before being put outside. In fact, it was soon found that the Zebra Finch was as happy in a cage as in an aviary, and it was also so hardy that not even the worst that a northerly climate could do would ruffle its feathers.

As has already been stated, this is a very active bird, and it is thus able to take sufficient exercise even in a small cage. Some hens, however, are prone to egg binding, and this may possibly have something to do with their being too closely confined. Exercise with short flights from perch to perch may be good enough for cocks, but it is possible that hens are fitter and less troubled by egg binding if, apart from the actual breeding season, they are allowed at least 6 ft. of flying space. When all is said and done, there is rarely any virtue in keeping birds too closely confined if it is in any way possible to provide more space for them.

The cheerfulness of the Zebra Finch is a characteristic which the owner soon learns about by watching his birds for a few minutes at a time. They are not only active, they are also "talkative," and this makes them really companionable. Practically all the time they are expressing vocally their interest in all that is going on around them. The notes they utter cannot be termed songs, for the Zebra Finch is no vocalist from the point of view of quality, yet the sounds are at least pleasant and do not grate upon the ear. It is customary to refer to the tiny "trumpet" tones of this small Australian finch, but when a number are housed together the sound is just like a crowd of gulls heard from

Finches

afar, so that distance has removed the harshness from their cries.

The Zebra Finch is not without its vices, but these are of a kind which can usually be controlled even if the bird's native instinct still remains the same. No bird could possibly be more inquisitive, and everything in either cage or aviary has to be inspected with great care.

The characteristic inquisitiveness is not a helpful quality in the breeding season, for no bird can make even the first attempt to build a nest without the Zebra Finch wanting to see for itself what is going on. Some birds are disturbed by this too-close attention, and when that is the case the Zebra Finch may have to be removed to other quarters.

When several pairs of these finches are kept together, there is always a good deal of harmless bickering over the choice of nesting sites, but no harm is done, and if there is a good choice of possible sites, all the pairs eventually find a place that suits them, and from that moment they settle down.

There is no difficulty in separating the sexes, for hens lack the chestnut cheek patches. The female also has no black barring on the breast, and her top color is a slightly duller shade of gray.

As a breeder the Zebra Finch leaves nothing to be desired, for it will breed in either cage or aviary and seems completely unconcerned by the receptacle provided for it. Of course, there is a right way and a wrong way

for the fancier to set about this business, but the fact still remains that most Zebra Finches will breed even when conditions cannot be regarded as ideal. There are, however, good pairs and bad pairs, but a small wooden box with a round hole in the side is usually sufficient to start any of these birds off, even if they do not see the business through to its logical conclusion.

As has already been stated, some hens seem prone to egg binding, and as soon as they are seen to be in trouble they must be given special treatment, and later be prevented from attempting to breed until they are obviously fit.

Another fact to be borne in mind is that the Zebra Finch, when once it starts to breed, is prepared to carry on all the year round, even during the depth of the winter. To allow this to happen would not be good for the adults nor for the consequent chicks, and the only thing to do with such a pair is to remove all the nest boxes when one feels that they have bred enough chicks for one season.

On the other hand, there are some pairs which display the most exasperating habit of building nest upon nest in the box, and as soon as each nest is complete the hen lays a clutch of eggs which are immediately covered. If a pair starts on this practice, they may not rear a single chick during the whole season. The birds which do act in this way just cannot see any nesting material without using it, and for them cage breeding is much more satisfactory with

52

Finches

only just enough material provided for a single nest. When such pairs are kept in an aviary with other birds, they are quite prepared to raid the nests of their companions in order to obtain additional material for their own purpose.

Although certain pairs do undoubtedly display this abnormal conduct, they must be regarded as the exception rather than the rule, for once a normal pair have built the nest, the hen lays her eggs and sits tightly until the chicks are hatched. Both parents will feed the brood with the greatest industry, and rear it successfully with little or no trouble.

The feeding of this finch presents no difficulty, for it is a plain eater and its needs are easily catered for. The seed it likes best is small yellow millet, and it will normally eat this before touching any other seed. However, variety in feeding is desirable, and white millet and canary should also be given. It is better to provide these three seeds in separate pots, as by adopting this method waste is prevented. Millet sprays should be given also, and although this is an expensive way of providing millet, it is well worth the extra expense.

Zebra Finches are very fond of green food and will eat this in considerable quantities, and both spinach and chickweed are prime favorites. When there are young in the nest, sprouted seed is a useful addition to their diet, but few show any interest in live foods.

Long-tailed Grass-Finch (*Poephila acuticauda*). Of all the Australian finches the Long-tailed Grass-Finch is probably the most popular, for although not brilliant in color, it is nevertheless very beautiful, and it is by no means as difficult to acclimate as that gem of Australian finches, the Gouldian.

The Long-tailed Grass-Finch is really hardy when it has settled down, and it can winter outdoors without heat if it is kept free from drafts and damp. Such conditions are not good for any birds, even those native to a country, and it is unwise to run any risks with foreign species which are used to an entirely different climate.

The Long-tailed Grass-Finch will be all the fitter during the following spring if it receives some form of protection during the winter months, and moderate artificial heat is useful. If the temperature of the shelter can be kept up to 50 F., the birds will be very comfortable and should come into breeding condition early the next year.

Long-tailed Grass-Finches are not troubled when they are kept confined in a cage, and soon they become quite steady. They will even breed in a cage, but it is unwise to keep them in anything less than 4 ft. long because the arrangement of the perches has to be borne in mind with these small birds which really do have, as their name implies, a long tail.

One of the great attractions of this species is the neatness of its plumage, which rarely looks ragged unless the

Finches

birds are overcrowded or kept in cages which are far too small. Even when the molt is near, the feathers will look almost as trim and tight as they did when the previous molt was completed months earlier. Sometimes the process of molting is so gradual that the appearance of the birds is hardly altered at all, and all the owner knows about this natural process is that he finds the feathers that have been dropped. Sometimes, however, the tail disappears in the course of a day, and then the Long-tailed Grass-Finch looks unusual for several weeks.

The sexes are so much alike that it is extremely difficult to separate them, and although there are certain clues which will help in making a decision, these are by no means reliable when taken separately. In the detailed description of this species these differences will be mentioned, but the final selection will usually have to be made on behavior. Even in this respect Long-tailed Grass-Finches are capable of deception when they are observed by the inexperienced fancier.

The beak is yellow and is usually at its brightest when the birds are in full breeding condition. Some cocks will be seen to have a more powerfully built beak than others, and it is possible also that, generally speaking, the beak of the cock is slightly larger than that of the hen. The difference between a cock with an ordinary-sized beak and a hen is so slight, however, that in itself it is not a reliable guide. Perhaps one can go no

further than to say that the really sturdily made beak is always found on a bird that is definitely a cock.

On the chin there starts the large black bib which is so characteristic of this species. It is frequently found that the bib of a cock is larger than that of the hen to which he is mated, but this is not always the case, for a cock and a hen may have bibs which are almost impossible to distinguish for size. Another fact that has to be remembered is that there is a definite tendency for this bib to increase slightly in size the longer the birds are kept in captivity.

It is extremely difficult to pass a general judgment on the Long-tailed Grass-Finch as a breeder, for it so often happens that two birds put together for breeding purposes are, in fact, of the same sex. Often, of course, this mistake is discovered and a pair is eventually found, but that does not mean that the birds will breed even if the cock goes to the extent of displaying. It is just one of those annoying habits which one sometimes encounters with these birds that they will display, and one feels certain that they will soon start to breed, whereas, in fact, they go no further with the business. There is some possibility of confusion even in the matter of the courtship display because sometimes both birds will sit opposite to each other and perform antics which are almost identical. One might suppose that these would be two cocks displaying, but it does happen also at times with pairs which have actually

Finches

bred and reared a family.

The owner has to be a very keen observer to distinguish a pair of this sort, but there are guiding principles that may resolve his doubts. If one bird persistently chases the other and yet shows no sign of spitefulness, it is the cock which is doing the chasing. Generally speaking, when the cock is waving his head backwards and forwards in front of the hen, often in the shape of a figure eight, he holds his head lower with his breast almost touching the perch. Hens are neither as quick in their bobbing and bowing movements, nor are they so persistent. The hen may show a temporary interest, but she will quickly tire of the whole proceeding, and it is then that the cock may start to chase her. Thus, careful observation is often necessary to be able to select a true pair.

From these somewhat derogatory remarks it must not be assumed that all Long-tailed Grass-Finches are bad breeders or hardened deceivers, for that would be far from the truth. Quite a good proportion are steady breeders, while not a few are really prolific, for they not only produce young but also rear as many as three broods during a single season.

These birds should not be put in a comparatively small aviary with other birds of their own or other species, for they are definitely inclined to be quarrelsome. This may not cause any serious damage either to themselves or the birds they attack, but it will definitely upset shy breeders of any species who will at once give up the task of attempting to produce a family.

Long-tailed Grass-Finches are not at all particular about the type of receptacle which they choose for the nest, but some pairs have a very distinct preference for some situations rather than others. On the whole, wire finch nests placed rather high up in the covered flight are likely to attract them, but they have often been known to scorn all the boxes or wire frames provided and to build high up in some bush in the aviary. Until they really get started on the nest they should be disturbed as little as possible, but when they have settled down they are not easily distracted from this task.

The material they like best for building a nest is a mixture of coarse and fine dried grass, but they also find grass roots of considerable help in holding the structure together. What they will actually choose as a lining is anyone's guess, but moss and feathers should both be provided. Both birds work together at the nest and make a structure which is reasonably neat, but always seems to contain far more material than is really necessary for the job in hand.

The color of the eggs is a pure white, and their number is normally four, but five or six is not in the least unusual. Any number in excess of this figure is often an indication that two hens have got together and deceived their owner by their courtship display. Had he kept

Finches

a careful eye on the black feathers of the bib, he would not have been hoodwinked in this fashion, for it is only the cocks who really puff out the feathers of the bib so that they stand almost erect at the time of the courting display.

Both birds take the business of incubation very seriously and share their duties with great regularity. It seems customary for the hen to cover the eggs at night, while the cock takes his turn when the lady comes off early in the morning. During the day, too, they may often be seen changing places, but the birds are so much alike that it is difficult to know which one is actually sitting at any particular moment. During the thirteen or fourteen days of incubation, the prospective parents are very careful to keep the nest tidy, and they have a habit of trying to conceal, at least in part, the entrance to the nest. This they do by adding extra material in this area, and it is not at all unusual to find the entrance completely concealed from the outside.

When the eggs hatch, both birds do the feeding, and they will then use those foods to which they are accustomed. They are not at all keen at this time to eat food which they do not have provided for them at other times of the year. Thus, if the owner wishes insects to form part of the youngsters' diet, the adults must be given such insects during the winter or early spring before they start to breed. Live foods have much to recommend them, but

they need not be regarded as essential, for many a brood of Long-tailed Grass-Finches has been reared without them.

Some very prolific pairs are bad feeders and are inclined to lose their chicks through inadequate feeding. This is probably due to the fact that they want to start breeding again far too soon after the first lot of chicks have hatched. If the birds feel this way, there is nothing that can be done about it, except perhaps to split the pair and provide each with a different mate. Fortunately this trouble is not frequently encountered, but it is a situation which has to be borne in mind.

If the parents are good feeders, the chicks will emerge from the nest in about a fortnight, but they still require feeding by their parents for about another week. Seeding grasses will attract the attention of the babies as soon as they can reach them. If in these early days the cock shows too much inclination to breed again, he should be removed for a few days. He should preferably be put out of earshot of the hen, for when a pair are separated they

*Photographs, pages 57-64: **57**—Star Finch cock (Neochmia ruficauda). **58**—Green Twinspot cock (Mandingoa nitidula). **59**—Fawn-and-White Bengalese (Society) Finch (Lonchura striata). **60**—Blue-breasted Cordonbleus (Uraeginthus angolensis). **62**—Masked Grass-Finch (Poephila personata). **63**—Fawn Zebra Finch cock (Poephila guttata). **64**—White-headed Nun (Lonchura maja).*

60

Finches

call to each other continuously. It is nearly always the cock who wishes to make a fresh start before his family have become independent. The chicks, when they are first fledged, are more or less gray all over, but they have dark tails. The underneath color is paler than the top, but at this early stage the feathers show little trace of pink.

Feeding this species is a simple matter, for the Long-tailed Grass-Finches can be trained to eat almost any type of food which would be considered suitable for finches. They are rather wasteful seed eaters, although they seem to like white millet, small yellow millet, and canary. It is better to provide these seeds in separate pots, for when this is done far less of the seed is scattered on the ground. Millet sprays are always very popular.

Seeding grasses are eaten eagerly and should be provided whenever possible, but these birds are rather more selective when it comes to other types of green food. The only thing to do is to provide them with as wide a choice as possible, and then let them take what attracts their fancy.

Live foods are a worthwhile addition to diet, but the Long-tailed Grass-Finch has conservative tastes, and experiment with these foods is necessary. Rarely will they refuse live ant cocoons, but unfortunately these are not easily obtained.

The Long-tailed Grass-Finch has hybridized with the Parson Finch, which is a closely allied species.

Gouldian Finch *(Chloebia gouldiae)*. There can be little doubt that the Gouldian Finch is one of the most beautiful exotic birds that a fancier has ever had the privilege of keeping in captivity, yet there are true bird lovers who regard the brilliance of coloring on this little bird as being so striking as to be almost garish. This is a severe judgment, but the colored areas are so sharply defined and separated that the coloring on the underside does appear a little harsh to the eye because there is so little blending.

The black-headed Gouldian Finch is the most common color morph in the wild. The red-headed Gouldian is even more striking in appearance, as is the uncommon yellow-headed. From the various reports of people who have made a study of this species in the field, the yellow-headed Gouldian seems to be entirely absent from some areas, and is apparently never more than two percent of the birds seen in a state of nature. The black-headed Gouldians are about four times as common as those with red heads. Perhaps this proportion would be somewhat less if the two colors mated among themselves in the wild, but as far as has been ascertained at present this crossing of colors does not normally take place. It may be that the birds select each other because they have a realization of color differences and choose a mate accordingly. In captivity color difference seems no bar to living together, mating, and later rearing a family.

Finches

These extremely beautiful birds, which are little more than 4 in. in length, come from tropical Australia and are found right across the country from west to east. They are always eagerly bought by bird lovers when they are in reasonable supply, although the price of a red-headed pair is still rather high. Any money spent on these birds, however, is well spent, provided that one has a certain amount of good fortune allied to experience. It must be admitted right from the start that the Gouldian Finch is difficult to acclimate, and throughout its life is inclined to be subject to several killing diseases, a state of affairs which presents a problem which up to the present has never been satisfactorily solved.

Gouldian Finches may be delicate and are certainly unpredictable, for they can become ill even after the shortest exposure to hard weather, or they can be full of life one day and yet lying dead on the bottom of the cage by the next morning. Yet gloomy though the prospects seem in theory for those who want to keep the Gouldian Finch, in practice the art of keeping them alive is not quite so difficult as it sounds, although it must be admitted that losses are above the average for seed-eating birds. It is rather strange that many seed eaters seem more subject to sudden illness than do most of the softbills when once they have become acclimated.

One fact should be accepted before this species is purchased. It is that the Gouldian Finch cannot stand harsh treatment, for the damp and drafts which are in the end fatal to most species affect Gouldians as soon as they are subjected to them. It is for this reason that this species should always be acclimated in a box-type cage which is at least 15 in. from back to front. This depth of cage allows the bird to get away from the front and well out of any drafts.

If a hospital cage is normally regarded by the aviculturist as a useful piece of equipment, for the keeper of the Gouldian Finch it is an absolute necessity. A bird which suddenly fluffs out its feathers and pokes its head under its wing has only one hope of survival and that is a high temperature at the very onset of the illness. If this heat is not provided, the birds will not feed, and it is remarkable how quickly they lose flesh and die from starvation. With newly imported birds there are a number of precautions which have to be borne in mind, and if these are known there are far greater chances of successful acclimation.

One thing which seems to upset these new arrivals is too much water to drink. Even now, when they travel by air, they are always thirsty when they reach the dealer and immediately make a dash for the water pots. If the dealer is wise, he will separate the birds into pairs and ration their water very strictly for the first fortnight. The bird keeper who buys a pair of Gouldians which have not been in the country long should always ask the dealer how long he has had them in stock. With this knowledge he will be better prepared to deal with the remaining period of acclimation.

Even when the birds are fully acclimated and reasonably hardy, great care has to be taken of them during the winter, and the temperature is best kept above 55 F., for they can develop pneumonia with apparent ease. Should they start to molt during the winter, they become extremely delicate, and then every effort should be made to keep them feeding heavily. A bird with flesh has reserves of energy when heavy demands are made on its stamina.

Now that the worst has been said about the Gouldian, the time has come to recommend it as an aviary bird to anyone who can afford to buy it, with the realization that the mortality rate is on the high side both for adults and young birds. As a cage bird it is ideal, provided that the cage is large enough, for it seems to like taking off in upward flight rather than horizontally. Thus, the cage should not be less than 2 ft. high, and an extra 6 in. in height will be a definite advantage. If Gouldians are inactive in a cage, this is usually because the cage is lacking in this necessary height. Activity is always of great importance in keeping these birds fit. When they are kept in outdoor aviaries, Gouldians need plenty of protection from wind and rain, and it is sound practice to have the side opposed to the prevailing wind fully boarded. A covered flight is always much better than an open one. Some successful breeders have only an open front to the flight.

The beak varies quite a lot in different specimens and also changes color on the same bird at different times of the year. Generally the beak is a pale horn tipped with red in the case of the black-headed and red-headed morphs, but on the beak of the yellow-head the tip is a dull orange, while the upper mandible itself is outlined in pale red. Sometimes the pale tone of the beak becomes much darker and assumes a more purple hue.

Hens are slightly smaller, for they only just exceed 4 in. in length, and are easily recognized by their much less bright colors. The breast alone of a hen would be sufficient evidence of her sex, for the deep violet of the cock is toned down to lilac, while the bright orange of the lower breast becomes no more than a pale yellow. In the red-headed morph the extent of the red is less on hens than on cocks, and the thin, but intense, black line which separates this band of color from the turquoise blue is much less distinct. The feet and legs of both birds are a pale mixture of pink and yellow which by a slight stretch of imagination could be called flesh color.

The Gouldian finch is a good breeder in captivity, and some pairs are so prolific that they have to be prevented from breeding or they would wear themselves out. The mating of one wild bird with another which has been bred in captivity is sound policy, but today the fancier must seek to buy aviary-bred birds which are unrelated. The fact that this is possible is in itself some proof of the comparative ease with which this species can be bred.

A word of caution is necessary to the inexperienced fancier before any attempt is made to persuade the birds to go to nest. Gouldian hens are very liable to egg binding, and it is more than likely that this is due to fanciers trying to breed with the birds too early in the year. The usual explanation given is that egg binding occurs because the temperature is too low and the muscles of the oviduct are cramped. An equally good reason might be that the hen is not in good condition because she has not been able to take sufficient exercise during the winter months. By holding the birds back until late in May, most of them will have got themselves into condition by flying in the fresh air, and egg binding ought to present no problem.

The male Gouldian is not one of those singers which can attract his mate's attention by the brilliance of his singing, for the best he can produce is a very gentle twitter. Nor, on the other hand, is he very active in his courtship display, yet normally he seems to think that the hen is ready to start nest building when he himself is so inclined. Often he is correct, and then immediately both birds set out to complete the task. At this time Gouldians are as peaceful as at any other time of the year, and several pairs can be quite safely bred together in the same aviary. If a large indoor cage is used, it is then probably more sensible to have only one pair to each cage.

The pair that has made up its mind to set about nest building looks quite carefully to find a suitable site, but almost invariably makes a choice of one of the open-fronted wooden nest boxes which have been provided. Perhaps Gouldians might prefer a hollow tree trunk, but the box usually appears adequately to satisfy their needs. As far as one can judge from observation, whim alone seems to dictate the particular nest box that is chosen.

The nest itself is spherical with an entrance in the side. With a few handfuls of soft hay thrown into the cage, the Gouldian has all it wants for nest building, as it shows no desire to use either moss, hair, or feathers as a lining. Usually, despite the simplicity of the nesting materials, the nest itself is very carefully woven.

A usual clutch is six eggs, but it is not at all uncommon to find one or more of these eggs infertile. Some hens develop an incurable desire to lay eggs and continue to lay several others even after they have started to sit tightly. The later eggs are usually infertile and are best removed, but it is essential that the birds have confidence in their owner before he embarks upon the liberty of disturbing them. If Gouldians are seriously disturbed, they are very likely to desert. When they are left alone, the hen gets on with her business by herself and receives very little assistance from the male. At the end of thirteen days the eggs should hatch, and from that time onwards both parents are busy, for feeding is a job which they take very seriously. It is a long business too, for the chicks rarely come out of the nest before the eighteenth day, and the period they spend in the nest after hatching may be as long as twenty-one days.

The young are green in color along the back, but this color lacks the brightness of the adults. Nor is this the only difference, for the head colors are missing, and there is no real sign of the brilliance of the breast and belly which will come when the birds are adult. One way in which the sex of young birds can be distinguished is the rather rapid development of the yellow on the lower breast of young cocks.

The feeding of the Gouldian Finch is of the greatest importance, for unless one is prepared to use all the wiles and arts of the experienced bird keeper, all that will be eaten will be canary and small yellow millet plus such seeding grasses as happen to attract their attention. Right from the start they should be got onto seeding grasses, for it is on these that they live very largely in the wild. Other green food should also be provided, and after a few trials chickweed and spinach will usually be readily accepted. Some Gouldians can be persuaded to take soft food and even insects, but others show no interest in these additions to what they themselves consider a normal diet. An occasional drop of ABDEC or other vitamin

compound in their drinking water will help to keep the birds fit.

Even when they are feeding a family, Gouldians show no great anxiety for live food, but if success is to be achieved, millet sprays are essential. Probably it is wise to provide millet in spray form all the time and sometimes to soak these sprays before feeding them. Grasses and small millet, however, remain the real essentials.

Red-headed Parrot-Finch *(Erythrura psittacea)*. Although the Red-headed Parrot Finch is not an exotic that is easily obtained, and even on the rare occasions when it is available it is expensive, it still deserves a full description of both its appearance and its habits, for it is a most attractive species which comes from the New Caledonia area.

The Red-headed Parrot-Finch has been imported on a number of occasions and has not proved difficult to acclimate, and with reasonable care has soon become quite hardy. This species, however, is too valuable to be exposed to undue risks, and it should receive some heat during the winter so that the temperature of the aviary shelter or cage is kept just above 50 F.

One unfortunate characteristic is its unsteadiness in a cage where, if it is surprised, it may stun itself by flying violently up against the top of the cage. Patience will soon cause it to become less nervous, but this parrot-finch never becomes really tame, and can never be persuaded to show any trust in its owner even at feeding time. The young are even more easily upset, and although they may be accommodated in a large aviary, will panic at the approach of persons whom they ought to recognize.

As this is a sturdy little bird in appearance, the fancier is not likely to associate it with species smaller than itself, but even if this were done, the Red-headed Parrot-Finch would not show the slightest signs of aggression. In some ways it is too timid, for at the least sign of interference by any other birds it will at once disappear to hide itself. It rarely comes to any harm because no breeder with any bird sense would think of putting such a gentle and also expensive bird with others which were likely to attack it so seriously as to cause real damage.

As an aviary bird it is very attractive, for it is extremely active, and if not frightened flits about in the most cheerful manner. Unfortunately it is not seen at its best in a planted aviary, for its outline is lost against the greenery of the plants, a large part of its plumage being green.

The sexes are so much alike that it is almost impossible to distinguish them from appearance, and from practically every point of view it is cheaper and more satisfactory in other ways also to try to buy a pair that have already bred. To be able to do this may take a long time, but it is well worth waiting.

When this parrot-finch was imported in reasonable numbers, there were always more cocks than hens according to those who bought them, but this may have been a mistaken idea drawn from the fact that the so-called pair did not breed.

The cock is not a singer, and is on the whole a quiet bird who is not often prepared to give away his sex by his vocal activities, and his quaint, whistling note is much more likely to be uttered when he thinks that he is not being observed. When he knows that he is being looked at, he is much more likely to remain silent, a fact which does not make sexing any easier. Here again patience will ultimately supply the answer if one does not know the sex of the birds that have been bought, for the hen never makes the slightest attempt to sing.

It has been stated on a number of occasions that hens show less red on the face than cocks, but this is not a very safe way of sexing the birds, for although some hens do show less scarlet on the forehead and throat than do cocks, it is not wise to say more than that. The young, when they first come from the nest, are a dull green with perhaps a few red feathers on the face or tail.

As a breeder the Red-headed Parrot-Finch can be a most exasperating bird, for apparent pairs may not show the slightest inclination even to build a nest. When this is the pattern of their behavior, it may be that one has two hens together, for two cocks have, in fact, been known to build a nest quite

Finches

happily, although that was the end of the story. Somewhat remarkably two hens do not attempt to build.

When one knows that there is a true pair in the aviary, it may not be difficult to persuade them to nest in either a wire finch frame or a box. This nest building is interesting, for there usually seems to be a remarkable division of labor with the cock collecting most of the material while the hen does most of the actual building. The completed nest is not very neat, but is rather sparrowlike with grass and straw and feathers as the chief materials. When it is finished it is certainly a solid structure, even if it lacks elegance.

Some cocks seem to be lacking in virility from the point of view of fertilizing the eggs, and it is comparatively unusual for the first clutch to be fertile. Whether the hen senses that these eggs are worthless is impossible to say, but it is not unusual for her to cover the first clutch with a further layer of nesting material and then to lay a second clutch on top.

It is important that the Red-headed Parrot-Finch should be allowed to nest in a secluded spot, for it is very easily disturbed, and if this happens the pair may desert at once. It is not only humans which can cause this trouble, for even other birds in the aviary which take too close an interest in what is going on can cause the parrot-finches to give up. This fact may be linked up with their habits in the wild where they are accustomed to build in holes so that

there is no direct view of the nest from outside.

If the birds settle down to nesting, they should be left undisturbed with no attempt on the part of the owner to see how many eggs have been laid, nor later should he try to find out when the chicks have hatched.

The clutch may be as few as three or as many as six eggs, and it is more than likely that at least one egg will be clear. The period of incubation is roughly a fortnight, and after that the chicks will remain in the nest for anything from nineteen to twenty-three days. When they do finally emerge, they will be self-supporting as soon as they can be persuaded to eat spray millet, and this usually happens in the course of the first three or four days.

Parrot-finches are plain feeders and do well on equal parts of canary, white millet, and yellow millet with the addition of millet sprays. Some of them discard quite a lot of white millet, and for such pairs the proportion of this seed can be reduced. A dish containing a properly proportioned finch mixture will also give them great pleasure.

Green food should be provided in variety, but they will be found to show a preference for the more fleshy type of leaf rather than seeding grasses. Chickweed and spinach are both popular.

Live foods may be eaten, but the Red-headed Parrot-Finch seems little interested in anything alive except the occasional mealworm. Even when

Munias

All of the munias seem more sturdily built than the waxbills and have more powerful beaks, although not all of them have beaks which are also short. The short, thick-set beak is characteristic of only a few species. However, there are some definite similarities between the birds described here, for they all have comparatively short wings which are inclined to be rounded. From this fact it follows that they are not particularly graceful in flight, but it does not imply that they are also inactive, for, in fact, they always seem to be on the move. Experience will show that they are restless birds which seem to be most happy when they are in a really large aviary, but miserable when confined in a cage.

The munias come both from Africa and from the Far East. In appearance these birds always seem neat in feather, but they are not brightly colored, although it often happens that the pattern of their rather sombre colors is most attractive to the eye.

There is not a real singer among them, but during the breeding season the cocks of some species make really valiant attempts to sing even if the result is no more than amusing.

As a group they are hardy and easy to keep in good condition, for they are not fussy feeders, and those that will breed in captivity are capable of performing this task on a mixture of seed and green foods; but by no means all of them are free breeders in captivity.

rearing young they do not show any greater interest in insects than at normal times.

The Red-headed Parrot-Finch, however, is rather partial to fruit of kinds that have not too much juice, and one finds that pears, when they are just ripe, are much appreciated. Apples may also be given, but they must not be sour.

There are several species of parrot-finch which have been imported, but the Red-headed, although rare, is the one most likely to be procurable, probably because some pairs are always good breeders if not actually prolific.

Blue-faced Parrot-finch (*Erythrura trichroa*). This parrot-finch has been imported on a number of occasions, but it is not as beautiful as the Red-headed species. It has a blue face and head. The back and throat are a dull green which turns to a brown green on the belly. On the rump the color is a dull red brown, but it is brighter than the tail.

This species should be fed and housed in the same way as the Red-headed Parrot-Finch, and if an enthusiast is lucky enough to be able to buy a pair, he will find these birds easy to manage when once they have become acclimated.

Munias

Some are called nuns, some mannikins, others finches, and so forth; but all are members of a group which has been accepted as one to be generally called the munias.

Bengalese Finch *(Lonchura striata).* The Bengalese, or Society, Finch is probably one of the most charming exotics that one can keep, for it not only has an ideal temperament but is also very easy to manage.

Bengalese are bred quite extensively in this country, on the Continent and in the United States, but in all of these areas only three varieties are readily available. The three common varieties are the White, the Chocolate-and-White, and the Fawn-and-White, but in addition to these there are crested birds which are not so common nor so popular as the others. For most fanciers the all-white holds the most attraction.

Acclimation is not necessary, for the birds have been bred in captivity for many generations, and they will settle down in new quarters without any trouble. In fact, they can be regarded as birds which have long become domesticated in the country in which they are purchased.

Probably they are better as cage birds than as inmates of an aviary, for they are extremely steady when caged and quickly become confiding. It is rather remarkable that birds which show no fear of humans should be so difficult to persuade to become hand-tame, but it is a work of great patience to get to the stage where a Bengalese will take food from the fingers.

If it is decided to put these birds outside with a collection of other species, the Bengalese will be found most friendly. They are never aggressive, and are even prepared to allow smaller birds to attack them without becoming spiteful themselves in return. Actually, they come to no harm, for they just get out of the way of unpleasant companions which are probably deterred from further aggression by the very sturdy beak of the Bengalese.

In shape the Bengalese is very similar to the Java Sparrow, except that the beak is not quite as stoutly built, while the bird itself is very little larger in size than the well-known Zebra Finch. The color pattern of the birds showing chocolate or fawn is by no means regular, and the patching assumes different patterns on different birds. Some are more heavily marked than others.

There are no sex characteristics which can be easily observed, and it is indeed a difficult task to pick out a true pair. Quite a number of Bengalese enthusiasts have put forward methods of choosing cocks or hens, but the suggestions put forward have not proved to be too reliable. There may be something in the theory that the hen is less wide across the base of the beak than the cock, but the difference is so small that it would require an expert to appreciate it. Another theory which has been put forward refers to the posture of the

Munias

birds when perching. If it is a guide, it is a difficult one to apply with any real degree of certainty.

The ordinary fancier will be well advised to buy a "true pair" from an expert, which in this case means two birds which have bred together and produced chicks. Such birds are naturally more expensive to buy, but they may prove to be cheaper in the long run, and may also save a great deal of time by making it unnecessary to pair up a number of birds.

Behavior is the only sure guide to sex, and even this breaks down on those very rare occasions when a hen decides to imitate the actions of a cock. As this is a very rare occurrence indeed, one need not bother about it further here, except to point out that a "pair" which does not breed may contain one of these unnatural hens.

Cocks do try to sing, whereas hens are more or less silent all the time, unless they are separated from their mates, when they will call to them. If the birds are caged separately it will be noticed that the call note of the sexes is quite different. The trouble with this method of sexing is that unless the pair have been together for some time and know each other well, they may not even bother to call at all.

Males are very fond of displaying, and if you happen to notice one of the birds with a piece of grass in its beak, it is a good idea to continue to watch, for this collecting of grass may be the prelude to a display which will establish the fact

that the bird concerned is a cock. If he returns to the perch and hops up and down on it while he also bows frequently and waves his head from side to side, you can feel confident that you have found your male. It is also most unusual for a cock to display unless the other bird is a hen.

Once a pair has been selected, the rest is easy, for Bengalese are free breeders and are likely to try to produce more families than is good for either them or their progeny. After three rounds of chicks the nest boxes should be taken away until the next season, for it is useless to produce chicks which are lacking in stamina.

These birds will breed equally well in either a cage or an aviary, and, as many fanciers have to keep their birds in cages, a species which will breed under these conditions is very valuable and of great interest.

Boxes 5 in. or 6 in. in cube are excellent receptacles for the nest, but it is unwise to use anything larger, for no matter how large the box, the Bengalese will try to fill it. The front of the nest box should be open except for the bottom third, which is left solid to keep in the nesting materials. Hay, coarse grass, and fine grass are all used for the building of this nest, and both birds work together at the task until the outside walls are completed. When this stage is reached, the hen spends more of her time on the inside while the cock remains outside making everything neat and tidy. The nest is lined with feathers, and with these a very soft bed is made for the eggs.

Once the nest is completed, both birds spend a good deal of time in it, and at this moment it is wiser to leave them alone than to look frequently to see whether the first egg has been laid. These eggs are pure white, and the number laid to complete the clutch may be four, five, or six. The hen will probably do most of the sitting, but the cock is often in the nest with her, and sometimes will be noticed actually covering the eggs. Hatching takes place in twelve to thirteen days, and it will be quite obvious when the young have arrived, for the parents are ideal feeders and will be seen constantly carrying food to their young.

As well as hatching their own eggs, which they do very satisfactorily if the eggs are fertile, the Bengalese is the ideal foster parent. A pair will usually accept the eggs of rarer birds in place of their own, and will thus often complete a breeding cycle which would otherwise be impossible. An occasional pair will turn out the "foreign" eggs or refuse to sit when these have been substituted for their own, but this occurrence is rare unless there is a considerable difference in the size of the eggs foisted upon them. They do not seem to mind any difference in color, although their own eggs are pure white.

Some pairs of Bengalese will also act as foster parents to the chicks of other species, but they are not as reliable when this is the form that the substitution takes. The only real chance of success seems to exist when the chicks of both pairs hatch almost at the same time. Naturally, they are not likely to be as successful with the offspring of birds which feed their young entirely on live foods, but even although they are largely seed eaters themselves, they will eat some live foods, and may be persuaded sometimes to rear chicks on a mixed diet.

The seeds they like best are white and also small yellow millet, and their preference seems to vary for these almost from day to day, so both should be given in separate pots to prevent any real waste. Seeding grasses are liked and should be given whenever possible, but, when these are not available, they are prepared to eat almost any form of green food, and to satisfy their whims a good deal of variety should always be provided. Chickweed and spinach are never refused, and Bengalese keep in much better condition if green food is given with great regularity. Some will eat apple and pear, but few are interested in the more fleshy fruits, though the unusual Bengalese may develop a passion for small white grapes provided that they are sweet.

Normally they are not very keen on insects, although some of them will eat chopped-up mealworms, and none of them ever seems able to refuse small spiders or live ant cocoons. Unfortunately, neither of these desirable foods is easily obtained. If they have a family to rear, especially when it is not their own, they should be offered the widest possible choice of food, including a really first-class insectile mixture with canary-rearing foods as a supplement to their diet.

Bengalese are reasonably hardy, but should be caged indoors during the winter months or they will be out of condition early in the following spring.

Black-headed Nun (Chestnut Munia, *Lonchura malacca atricapilla).* This is a most attractive munia from India and Indochina, which is very freely imported. It is such a common bird that it has been given several popular names, of which the Black-headed Nun is the one most frequently used. The description chestnut-bellied does not really fit it, for the belly itself is black and it is only the flanks that are chestnut in color. Taking the body as a whole, there is a greater area showing a chocolate color than black, although in common with quite a number of other similar birds it does actually have a head that is black.

A most noticeable feature about it is the neatness of its plumage, due undoubtedly to the fact that it spends a good deal of time each day on preening. It is for this reason that it should be provided with a bath daily, for no bird can really do a great deal about the preening of its feathers unless bathing facilities are provided with great regularity and frequency.

Even in the days when the Black-headed Nun had to undergo a long sea journey before it arrived in this country, it was always smart in appearance when it reached the dealer. With the more rapid methods of transport today, it is surprising, but nevertheless true, that it frequently does not arrive in such good feather because it has been overcrowded. If it is given an immediate opportunity of bathing, it soon looks neat and tidy once again.

One of its greatest virtues is its friendliness with other birds, and it never becomes aggressive towards them even when it is provoked. Unfortunately, this friendliness is not shown to those who look after it, for it is extremely shy and tries to hide itself away in the aviary in places where it cannot be seen. It is not at all strong on the wing, and for that reason, when kept outside in an aviary, there should be plenty of bushes so that it can hop from branch to branch. Otherwise it will spend too much time on the ground or hanging from the wire, where its neat tail will be quickly ruined. These facts may constitute a strong argument for turning the Black-headed Nun into a cage bird, for there it will hop happily from perch to perch, and, even if it never becomes actually tame, and it rarely does, it soon becomes reasonably steady, because it eventually realizes that no harm will come to it.

It is a pity that it does not show itself off to advantage in an aviary, for it is extremely hardy, and, if kept in dry quarters, can tolerate really low temperatures without coming to any harm. When the weather is really cold, it should still be given water for bathing, and if afterwards it is able to take ample exercise it will not suffer from this Spartan treatment.

The sexes are absolutely alike in coloring and shape, and it is thus very difficult to find a pair. It is probably for this reason that it has been found so difficult to get these birds even to build a nest, which is merely the first stage in the founding of a new generation, but this is by no means the only reason.

Perhaps if it could be arranged that a colony of these birds were kept together in a large, naturally planted aviary, there would be more records of successful breeding, for in the wild it is without doubt gregarious, and in this state of nature birds live happily together in colonies of considerable size. In captivity the Black-headed Nun is usually found in mixed collections of small birds where only one or two "pairs" are kept together. It is safe even with the smallest waxbills, but it will show little inclination to breed in such company.

The only way that cocks can be recognized is by their song or perhaps rather by the violent efforts they make to produce one. A cock will stretch his neck to its fullest extent, while his throat works with the greatest energy. Yet the sound which emerges is scarcely audible.

A few fortunate fanciers may find a pair which will set to work to build a spherical nest of dried grass. This nest is not very carefully built, but the structure is workmanlike enough and will hold the eggs if they are laid. For this stage to be reached, however, is even more rare. So the Black-headed Nun must be regarded as a bird that does not breed successfully in captivity.

The seed mixture should be small yellow millet and canary, for white millet is rarely appreciated, as this little bird seems to find difficulty in removing the husks.

As far as one can observe in a mixed collection, the Black-headed Nun does not eat any of the ordinary live foods, but it may eat very small insects which it finds for itself on the growing plants. In a cage it will not look at live foods, however tempting these may be to any other small birds that are kept with it. Seeding grasses and green oats are eaten with great appetite, but when these are not available it is more often than not impossible to persuade the Black-headed Nun to eat any green food at all.

Tri-colored Nun (Chestnut Munia, *Lonchura malacca malacca).* The Tri-colored Nun comes from India and Ceylon, and has been imported on many occasions, although it has never been a common bird in aviaries in this country.

The three colors which are found on this bird make it most attractive in appearance, for it has a black head, throat, and belly, with all the rest of the plumage chestnut except that the breast and flank are a pure white.

It is in size a little larger than the Black-headed Nun, but is just as gentle

Munias

in its behavior toward other birds and never makes a nuisance of itself.

Some fanciers may have bred it in captivity, but it has always been extremely difficult to obtain pairs, as the number of birds imported has never been large, with the result that knowledge of its attempts to breed are very limited.

White-Headed Nun (*Lonchura maja*). This bird is similar in many respects to the Black-headed Nun, its only really distinguishing feature being the off-white color of the head, for in most other respects the two species are almost identical in appearance and certainly in behavior.

There are some slight yet observable differences in the manner in which the colors are arranged on the bird, for on the Black-headed Nun the line of demarcation between the black and the chestnut is very clearly defined, while on the White-headed there is a gradual shading from white to chestnut. The belly color too shows a difference in the White-headed, for in this area the feathers are not white as one would expect, but the plumage is distinctly brown, and considerably darker on the sides than in the middle.

In many ways the White-headed is not as attractive as its more common relative with a black head, perhaps because in appearance it is not so striking, and if there is any difference in behavior, it is that this species is even more shy. When living in the wild it feeds very largely on rice, and sometimes it does not take too kindly to the seed mixtures available for cage or aviary birds. When it is first received, it may be difficult to persuade it to eat anything, and, as it is certainly not a hardy species and seems to be somewhat lacking in stamina, it is therefore more difficult to acclimate. A little patience, however, will soon get it onto a satisfactory diet.

There have been very occasional reports that it has been bred in captivity, but there can be no doubt about the difficulty of breeding this species.

Indian Silverbill (*Lonchura malabarica*), **African Silverbill** (*Lonchura cantans*). There are two species of silverbills well known to exotic bird fanciers. One is of African origin and the other comes from India. In appearance they are very much alike,

White-headed Nun (Lonchura maja).

although there is no possibility of confusing them, but they are so closely related that they can actually be bred together.

One point of great interest attached to these birds is the fact that they will breed in a cage, which is by no means the case with the majority of exotic birds imported into this country. Thus, the fancier who wants to breed exotics has here two species which he can put together hopefully, even if he has no outside aviary for his birds. Both species are free breeders if one is fortunate enough to obtain a good pair, but it has to be admitted that there are some pairs that never attempt to breed.

When this is the case, it is wise first of all to come to the conclusion that two birds of the same sex have been put together, and even fanciers of considerable experience will admit that the sexes are so much alike that it is almost, if not quite, impossible to select them on appearance alone. It will be noticed that some hens do, in fact, possess heads which are slightly more refined than those of cocks, but this is not always the case. In size the sexes are alike, and it is only with a hen that has laid eggs that one is likely to see any color difference at all.

The cocks of both species do sing, and this is the surest way of sexing them. Even here, however, there is a complication, for they do not sing all the year round, but confine their vocal efforts largely to the breeding season. There is also another useful hint from the birds themselves if one is prepared to observe them carefully for a time. Some cocks select particular hens for themselves, and, if a dozen birds are kept in a large cage, it will be noticed that certain individuals make a habit of picking another bird as a partner. This self-selected pair can often be seen perching together during the day and almost invariably at night. If there are a number of perches at the same level, some pairs are very likely to separate themselves in this fashion. But if a fancier cannot afford to buy a dozen birds, by far the safest thing to do is to rely upon a breeder who has a "true" pair for sale.

Silverbills are hardy birds and present no serious difficulty when they are first imported, provided they are in good condition on arrival.

However, the hardiness of the silverbill is such that it will soon recover if it is given good treatment. A point to remember here is that silverbills are very fond of seeding grasses, and a bunch of these will quickly put them onto food, which is the important first step.

On the whole, the silverbill is rather a timid bird, and when breeding will quickly desert if it is disturbed. Although the Indian species is almost 5 in. in length, it can be safely housed with even the smallest birds, for it is never aggressive. It is, in fact, so good-natured that it will allow itself to be harassed by these smaller birds without reprisal. Actually, very little harm ever happens to the silverbill, for its size demands some respect from most small birds, although they cannot know that there will be no counter-action even if they are a nuisance.

In a cage it becomes steady and learns to know the person who cares for it, but if it is to be bred in a cage, great care has to be taken to see that it is not disturbed. It is movement rather than sound that upsets it, and thus, if the cage is kept in a living-room, it is a sensible plan to cover with cardboard that part of the front behind which the nest box will be suspended. The cock, which often stands guard on top of the nest box, is the one who seems to cause the alarm when the hen comes dashing out of the nest. Frequently his warning is quite unnecessary.

Silverbills will build a nest in either a box or a wire finch frame, and do not seem to mind what materials they use. In fact, if the normal materials are not provided for them, they will try to construct a nest from anything they can find in the aviary. When there is a plentiful supply of coarse and fine dried grass, with some feathers, they will be completely happy and at once set to work. At first both of them work together, but after a time the cock grows tired and contents himself with perching on top of the nest and from there directing the operations. Feathers are used finally as a lining for the nest and a bed for the eggs.

These eggs are pure white in color and vary in number from four to six, but the usual number is five. It is the hen that does the incubating, although from time to time the cock may go into the spherical nest when the hen has come off to feed. He may stand among the eggs, but he does not seem to be sitting on them. Closer inspection is not advisable to find out what is really happening, or there may be some broken eggs, as a cock in this position is easily alarmed. Incubation lasts about twelve days, and from then on both parents start to feed the chicks, but in this task the hen is always the harder worker. In the wild, silverbills feed largely on wild seeds, and in captivity they do very well on small yellow millet with about half as much white millet added. Some will eat canary if it is small, but others show no interest in it at all. Silverbills are certainly fond of seeding grasses, and also a variety of green foods including lettuce, spinach, and dandelion, but too much of the last-named is not good for them.

How much insect life silverbills eat in the wild is probably not known, but when kept in captivity some of them display a keen appetite for small insects, including mealworms. Gentles may also be eaten, but often they are evacuated apparently undigested. Many silverbills will not touch insects at any time, apart from small flying creatures which they catch for themselves in the aviary. There need be no anxiety if a breeding pair refuse all live foods, for they can rear their families quite satisfactorily on a purely vegetarian diet.